For Hannah —
a woman who is...

Precious in His Sight

The Fine Art of Becoming a Godly Woman

By
PAT ENNIS

Pat Ennis 🙂
1 Peter 3:3-4.

Published by

TrustedBooks

BOOKS YOU CAN DEPEND ON

a division of VMI Publishers
Sisters, Oregon
www.vmipublishers.com

ISBN: 1-933204-26-5
Library of Congress Control Number: 2006929963

Author Contact: drennis@masters.edu

Dedicated to

Dr. Barbara M. Schuch
with gratitude for your enduring
friendship throughout the years.
God's blessing on you, dear friend!

Contents

The Godly Woman and Her Emotions

Precious in His Sight Is the Woman Who:

Acknowledgments

This is one of my favorite pages of the book because I am able to affirm many of the individuals who supported the creation of *Precious in His Sight: The Fine Art of Becoming a Godly Woman*. Among them I offer special gratitude to:

Bill and Nancie Carmichael—Your enthusiasm for *Precious in His Sight: The Fine Art of Becoming a Godly Woman* was evident from our initial contact. Thank you for presenting my manuscript to the editorial committee, responding to myriad questions, and seeing the project through to its completion.

Carella DeVol—Your moral support, enthusiasm, and consistent prayer on all aspects of my ministry is a consistent encouragement.

Kathy Ide—What a privilege to have you as my editor. Thank you for your affirming words and for adhering to a high standard of excellence throughout the editing process.

Laura Leathers and Donna Morley—Your prayer support, encouragement, and wisdom throughout the writing process was a source of joy.

Lacey Hanes Ogle—Thank you for always graciously responding to my questions.

Stacy Oliver and Nancie Carmichael—Who endorsed not only the content of *Precious in His Sight: The Fine Art of Becoming a Godly Woman* but also my character.

Dr. Barbara Schuch—Your unselfish sharing of your editorial skills, thought-provoking comments, and belief in Precious in His Sight provided momentum to keep the project in process.

Leanne Throop—For your diligence in working with the formatting and various versions of the Bible.

The VMI Team—Your commitment to excellence made this partnership in the ministry of the written word a joy.

My Gracious Heavenly Father—You established the criteria for successful womanhood in Your Holy Word and then provided the strength to apply it to daily living. Eternity will not be long enough for me to express my love and gratitude to You!

Precious in His Sight:
The Fine Art of Becoming a Godly Woman

Introduction

Women often ask me, "How do I know if I am pleasing my heavenly Father?" They anticipate a deep theological or even mystical response to come forth from my lips. However, my response is generally something like, "God's will for your life and mine is found in 1 Peter 3:4. We are to do whatever is necessary to cultivate 'the hidden person of the heart, with the imperishable quality of a gentle and quiet spirit, which is precious in the sight of God'" (NASB). *Gentle* means "meek or humble" and quiet describes the character of a woman's actions and reactions to her husband and to life in general. Such a spirit is precious not only to her husband, but also to God.[1]

I do not have to demonstrate a lack of backbone, nor be like a rag doll that flops about. Rather, I am to exhibit strength under the control of the Holy Spirit (Galatians 5:22-23). This type of behavior demonstrates a gentle and quiet spirit, which is precious in His sight. [2]

Precious in His Sight: The Fine Art of Becoming a Godly Woman was written to allow you to spend time in your heavenly Father's company, cultivating character qualities that contribute to the development of a gentle and quiet spirit. The topics for the chapters are drawn from the spiritual challenges that I, as well as women I have taught and counseled through my spiritual pilgrimage, confront. As the unchanging Word of God is applied to our lives, we become victors rather than victims—and in the process, experience growth toward a gentle and quiet spirit.

So I invite you to open your heart to the Scriptures—God's special instructions to His children. Saturate your mind with His thoughts, examine the lives of women who are recorded on the pages of His Word, and meditate on principles designed to assist you in developing the type of spirit that is precious in our heavenly Father's sight. I urge you to consider using the "Developing a Gentle and Quiet Spirit" guidelines found at the conclusion of each chapter to reinforce what it teaches.

It is my prayer that *Precious in His Sight: The Fine Art of Becoming a Godly Woman* will launch for you a lifelong quest of developing character qualities that contribute to the development of a gentle and quiet spirit. Begin today and anticipate, with joy, the deepening of your relationship with your heavenly Father (Jeremiah 31:3).

The Godly Woman and Her Spiritual Life
Precious in His Sight is the Woman Who:

1. Understands Her Physical and Spiritual Nutritional Requirements
2. Chooses to Be a Victor in the Midst of Testing
3. Cultivates Spiritual Vitality
4. Joyfully Uses Her Spiritual Gifts
5. Is Willing to Be Stretched to Communicate God's Message of Hope to Others
6. Wears Garments that Reflect Her Royal Heritage
7. Understands Singleness from Her Heavenly Father's Perspective
8. Models Her Heavenly Father's Character
9. Chooses to Evaluate Her Spiritual Growth

1

Precious in His Sight is...

The Woman Who Understands Her Physical and Spiritual Nutritional Requirements

A new opportunity for study is upon you. It is filled with the potential to deepen your relationship with your heavenly Father and to increase your ability to fulfill the special plan He has just for you. You are more likely to fulfill that plan if you are spiritually and physically fit.

How are you beginning your first day of this study? Are you approaching it with a solid understanding of the nutritional requirements necessary for spiritual and physical vitality? Or are you starting it randomly, without a deliberate dietary plan?

Physical Dietary Plan

Physically, you know that your body has specific nutritional requirements in order to function properly. When you stand on the scale and observe the weight that it records, your response may be, "I surely have more than fulfilled those requirements in the past, and now it is time for me to consider a diet—a new plan for my nutritional intake."

As you review your knowledge of nutrition, you know that a variety of foods are necessary to nourish you—meats, eggs, grain foods (breads, cereals, pastas), fruits, vegetables, and dairy products, as well as fats, oils, and sugars in moderate amounts. No one food is more or less important than the others; they are all needed and they all help one another nourish you. (Reread Genesis 1 as a reminder that each act of creation concludes with the statement, "And God saw that it was good.")

Meats and eggs supply the protein necessary to build strong bodies and maintain body tissue. They are also an abundant source of iron needed for rich red blood and the prevention of anemia, as well as the essential B vitamins. The word *protein* comes from the Greek for "first" and should be the first criteria when planning meals. The grain foods supply vigor and energy because of the carbohydrates, sugars, and starches they contain as well as significant amounts of the B vitamins, thiamine, niacin, and riboflavin.

Our gracious heavenly Father packaged some of our best cosmetics in the fruits and vegetables He created. Rather than beauty coming from jars, tubes, and fancy bottles, a healthy glow from within, the source of true beauty, is the result of a diet that abounds in the beauty foods—fruits and vegetables. A healthy body silhouette is a combination of balancing proteins, fats, and carbohydrates with plenty of low-calorie fruits and vegetables complemented with exercise.

Dairy products build and maintain bones and teeth; the calcium and phosphorus contained in milk assists in calming the nerves. Their protein helps maintain body tissue while the fat supplies energy and vitamin A for sound growth and general health. Vitamin D-fortified milk supplements the "sunshine vitamin," which the body produces when exposed to the sun.

Fats, oils, and sugars are the "plus" foods. While they are to be used in moderation, each contributes some nutritive value to our diets. Fats and oils provide the body with energy, bring some of the important fat-soluble vitamins into our system, aid in digestion of essential foods, and endow our meals with full-bodied flavor. Sugar provides quick energy and helps the body utilize other nutrients, although its most obvious contribution is its taste, which makes many foods more appetizing.

Spiritual Dietary Plan

An intentional spiritual dietary plan is as essential to your spiritual growth as a deliberate dietary plan is fundamental to your physical well-being. First Peter 2:2-3 teaches that spiritual growth is marked by a craving for and a delight in God's Word, with the intensity with which a baby craves milk. A Christian develops a desire for the truth of God's Word by:

1. remembering his life's source
   "the word of the Lord endures forever" (1 Peter 1:25 NKJV)

2. eliminating sin from his life
   "therefore, laying aside all malice, all deceit, hypocrisy, envy, and all evil speaking" (1 Peter 2:1 NKJV)

3. admitting his need for God's truth
   "as newborn babes" (1 Peter 2:2 NKJV)

4. pursuing spiritual growth
   "that you may grow thereby" (1 Peter 2:2 NKJV)

5. surveying his blessings
   "the Lord is gracious" (1 Peter 2:3 NKJV)

When you make sound nutritional choices, you have the opportunity to dramatically reduce your risk for many health challenges. The same is true in your spiritual life. When you ingest a regular diet of God's Word, spiritual vitality results. According to Psalm 119, an excellent Spiritual Nutrition Guide, God's Word is your:

- source of blessing (vss. 1-8)
- challenge to holiness (vss. 9-16)
- teacher (vss. 17-24)
- source of strength and renewal (vss. 25-32)
- direction for life priorities (vss. 33-40)
- reminder of God's unfailing love (vss. 41-48)
- comfort in suffering (vss. 49-56)
- portion (vss. 57-64)
- standard for correction (vss. 65-72)
- source of consolation (vss. 73-80)

- hope for revival (vss. 81-88)
- unwavering standard (vss. 89-96)
- foundation for wisdom, understanding, and insight (vss.97-104)
- direction for life (vss. 105-112)
- shield (vss. 113-120)
- surety (vss. 121-128)
- starting point for understanding (vss. 129-136)
- reference for pure counsel (vss. 137-144)
- response to cries for help (vss. 145-152)
- deliverance (vss. 153-160)
- basis for peace (vss. 161-168)
- reason for praise (vss. 169-176)

As you proceed through *Precious in His Sight,* purpose, through our Lord's strength, to improve your physical and spiritual habits. Remember, precious in His sight is the woman who understands her physical and spiritual nutritional requirements.

Developing a Gentle and Quiet Spirit

Scriptures to Study

Deuteronomy 8:3; Psalm 119; Matthew 4:4; Luke 4:4;

2 Timothy 3:16

For Meditation

Psalm 119:11

For Further Study

- Carefully analyze Psalm 119 and list all the roles God's Word can fulfill in your life.

- Locate, memorize, and meditate on verses of Scripture that will help you refrain from sinning against your heavenly Father (Psalm 119:11).

- What do you learn from Mary's life, whose first priority was to spend time with her Lord so she could serve Him effectively, that will allow you to joyfully serve Him (Luke 10:38-42)?

A Principle to Ponder

Precious in His sight is the woman who filters her daily decisions through the changeless instructions found in God's Word (Psalm 119:9-16).

2

Precious in His Sight is...

The Woman Who Chooses to be a Victor
in the Midst Of Testing

As a college professor I have two primary responsibilities to my students. The first is to provide them with instruction in the subject-matter content, and the second is to determine whether or not they have mastered it. Their subject-matter mastery is usually measured in the form of a test—and it is always my desire that they will earn a high grade on it. I know, however, that for it to be a valid measurement, the test must be difficult enough to align with their academic maturity. I do them no favors if it is too easy, and it is not a reliable measurement if it is too difficult.

Spiritually I must be willing to apply the same testing principle to my life. When my gracious heavenly Father deems that I have mastered a biblical truth, it is likely that He will provide an opportunity for me to demonstrate my ability to apply it. This opportunity normally presents itself in the form of a test, and its purpose is to reveal the quality of my integration of the biblical truth into my life. It is comforting to know that my heavenly Father wants me to pass the test at the top of my class, not simply squeak by. In fact James 1:2-5 teaches me that the testing of my faith should produce deeper communion and greater trust in Christ—qualities that in turn produce a stable, godly, and righteous character.[4]

When you discern that your heavenly Father is testing you, do you anticipate being a victim or a victor? A *victim* is an individual who suffers from a destructive or injurious action and is deceived or cheated, while a *victor* is a person who has overcome or defeated an adversary.[5] Satan is your adversary, and he "prowls around like a roaring lion, seeking someone to devour" (1 Peter 5:8-9). Essentially, he is seeking opportunities to overwhelm you with temptation, persecution, and discouragement. If you succumb to his ploys, you become a victim; however, if you resist him and continue to live according to God's Word, you are a victor. James 4:7 instructs us to "submit yourselves therefore to God. Resist the devil, and he will flee from you." When you make the choice to submit to God, you are taking a stand against Satan, moving you from victim to victor status.

Numerous biblical teachings provide us with the formula for becoming a victor in the midst of life's tests. Let's examine several principles that emerge from a brief review of their contents:

- Your gracious heavenly Father tests you while Satan tempts you (1 Corinthians 10:13; James 1:13-15). Abraham stands as a stark example of having the sincerity of his faith tested as God asked him to sacrifice his long-awaited, promised son (Genesis 21:1-19).
- You are to make a concentrated effort to rejoice in the midst of the tests (James 1:2). Knowing this is impossible in your own strength, you must actively draw your strength from the Lord (Philippians 4:13).
- The testing of your faith produces endurance or perseverance, thus refining your character and providing a foundation for greater usefulness to our Lord's kingdom (Romans 5:3; James 1:3).
- Endurance is a command for believers, not a suggestion; its intended result is to refine character (James 1:4; 1 Peter 5:10).
- Though "fast food" does exist, there is no such commodity as "fast faith." Let's review several biblical role models who validate this principle:

1. Abraham and Sarah waited twenty-five years for Isaac (Genesis 17:19; 21:2).

2. It took Joseph thirteen years to get from the pit to the palace (Genesis 37-41).

3. Moses spent a number of years in leadership candidacy school (Exodus 2:11-3:22).

- Endurance does not come vicariously—you must proceed through the entire test to produce it. The Lord Jesus provides the ultimate example of remaining under the test through its completion (Hebrews 12:1-2).

- Though you may desire to be released from the test, your heavenly Father wants to take you through it so that you become a mature believer (Colossians 1:28; 4:12; James 1:4).

- Just as the refiner's fire assesses the quality of metal, so the genuineness your faith is assessed through tests (1 Peter. 1:7).

- If you are more interested in comfort than character, you will waste the test. However, if you fail it, your gracious heavenly Father will give you the opportunity to enroll in His remediation course (1 Corinthians 10:13).

Mary, the mother of Jesus, provides us with a wonderful example of approaching life's tests with the intention of being a victor rather than a victim. Let's examine her life in terms of the reasons for concern, her response, and the results.

- Reasons for concern (Luke 1:26-31)—God sent an angel to comfort Mary, who was greatly troubled because she was betrothed to Joseph and was aware of her fate if she was found to be pregnant (Deuteronomy 22:23-24). Additionally, she undoubtedly experienced some emotional turmoil at the thought of being the mother of the Son of God.

- Response (Luke 1:28-46)—Mary chose to be a victor in the situation by placing her future into the hands of her heavenly Father and declaring herself as the "servant of the Lord" (1:38a).

Her attitude was one of submission to her heavenly Father as she responded to the difficult test by stating, "Let it be to me according to your word" (1:38b). She chose to believe that her heavenly Father would work out the details—her responsibility was to trust (Proverbs 3:5-6; Romans 8:28). She chose to spend time with Elizabeth, an individual who would nurture her through the testing season (1:39-45).

- Results (Luke 1:46-56)—Mary's response reflects that her heart and mind were saturated with the word of God. Her ability to focus on the covenant promises of God provides an incredible role model for us—that of hiding God's Word in our lives so that when adversity strikes we have the spiritual ammunition to "extinguish all the flaming arrows of the evil one" (Ephesians 6:16 NASB; see also Psalms 1; 119:11; Jeremiah 17:7-8; Ephesians 6:10-20).

Perhaps you have already faced tests. If not, before you conclude this book, one or more will undoubtedly be a part of your life. Just as I want my students to conquer academic tests, so your gracious heavenly Father desires you to completely conquer all of your spiritual tests (Romans 8:31-39). The choice is yours. Will you follow Mary's role model and choose to be a victor, or consent to becoming a victim (1 Peter 5:6-9)?

Developing a Gentle and Quiet Spirit

Scriptures to Study

Luke 1:26-47

For Meditation

James 1:2-4

For Further Study

- Identify the fifteen verses of Scripture recorded in Luke 1:26-47 and their Old Testament source that Mary focused on during her test.

- When you discern that your heavenly Father is testing you, do you anticipate being a victim or a victor? Develop a testing strategy that allows you to successfully pass the tests. For example, one strategy might be "I will choose to count if all joy when I fall into various tests" (see James 1:2-4). Once the testing strategy is developed, purpose to implement it at the first sign of a test.

- What attitudes and actions did Mary, the mother of Jesus, exemplify that allowed her to be recorded as a handmaiden of the Lord (Luke 1:26-47)?

- List specific attitudes and actions that you have or need to cultivate so that your character is affirmed in the same way.

- Ask your heavenly Father to provide you with the strength to become His handmaiden (Philippians 4:13).

A Principle to Ponder

Precious in His sight is the woman who, in the midst of tests, chooses to be a victor rather than a victim (James 1:2-5).

3

Precious in His Sight is...
The Woman Who Cultivates Spiritual Vitality

$\mathcal{C}$ommencing my doctoral degree was a decision I agonized over. I entered higher education with a master's degree and the promise from my employer that my position would never be contingent on pursuing a doctorate. As the Home Economics program I developed blossomed and matured, however, I knew I would hinder its credibility if I maintained my reluctance to embark on a doctoral program.

A sabbatical to pursue the degree was impossible, so I enrolled in a program that could be completed concurrently with full-time employment. The one available in my area required coursework during the academic year and twenty weeks of residency on the Northern Arizona University campus that spanned three summers. The first summer I identified with Ruth the Moabitess (Ruth 1-4)—I left all that was familiar to reside in a foreign environment. During my devotion times that summer, our Lord allowed me to discover Jeremiah 17:7-8; subsequently, it became the motivating verse for my doctoral studies.

Sixteen hours of comprehensive examinations followed my coursework. I completed eight hours and found myself in extreme pain at the conclusion of the second. Diagnosis revealed gall bladder disease and surgery was scheduled. Prior to departing for the hospital, I packed my briefcase with the remaining notes I needed to commit to memory. During my seven days in the hospital, I consistently meditated on Jeremiah 17:7-8 for spiritual vitality and studied for the remaining examinations as my stamina permitted. My heavenly Father chose to allow my "leaf to be green" (see Jeremiah 17:8) though the heat was intense. I completed the examinations on time, and my written responses yielded academic fruit that exempted me from the oral portion.

Through this experience I was once again reminded that God's Word provides guidelines for possessing spiritual vitality in unforeseen circumstances. May I share with you some principles that emerged which continue to provide spiritual vitality for me?

- Ultimately, I have only two choices in life: obedience or rebellion to my heavenly Father's instructions. If I desire spiritual vitality, I will select obedience (Psalm 1:1).
- I experience deep joy and contentment, not simply a superficial happiness, when I choose to seek counsel from God's Word and godly individuals (Psalm1: 1).
- My friendships need to be cultivated from those who desire to lead a godly lifestyle (Psalm 1:1; Proverbs 1:10; 4:14, 7; 1 Timothy 4:6-7; 6:3-5).
- If I consistently internalize God's Word (Psalm 119:11), I will possess spiritual vitality (Psalm 1:2). This internalization process begins with spending time daily reading and thinking about the Scriptures, asking my heavenly Father how I should apply them to everyday life, purposing to be obedient through His strength, and joyfully responding to His instructions (Philippians 4:13).
- The more I internalize God's Word, the more its contents will influence my daily life (Psalm 1:2-3).
- My spiritual vitality is directly related to the thoughts I deposit in my memory bank—I can only withdraw what I have deposited (Psalm 1:2-3).

- The more I consume spiritual food (God's Word), the greater my spiritual appetite. As sound nutritional food choices lend themselves to my physical well-being, so wise spiritual food choices contribute to my spiritual vitality (Psalm 1:2-3).

- My fruitfulness is in direct proportion to the meditation and application of God's Word (Psalm 1:2-3).

- When I meditate on God's Word and apply it to my life, I am not guaranteed consistent prosperity or exemption from life's challenges. The prosperity that my heavenly Father does assure is peace in the midst of difficulty and attitudes that please Him (Psalm 1:3).

- The ability to receive God's abundant provision comes as I am transplanted from sin to salvation. Only when I experienced salvation did I acquire the capacity to achieve long-term spiritual vitality (Psalm 1:3).

- I have a responsibility to appropriate the abundant resources of God so that I possess spiritual vitality regardless of outward circumstances (Psalm 1:3; Jeremiah 17:8).

- A life that displays spiritual vitality will bear fruit, even under difficult circumstances. A life lacking spiritual vitality is comparable to chaff—the outer shell that must be removed to release the valuable kernels of grain. Chaff is lightweight and is carried away by the slightest wind, while the quality kernel that drops to the earth germinates, eventually producing a quality harvest. I make the choice to be like chaff or grain kernels when the winds of adversity blow (Psalm 1:3-4).

- I must avoid any practice that would place me in the category of an ungodly individual (Psalm 1:4).

- My choices, lifestyle, and appetites reveal my spiritual vitality. When I choose to refrain from every appearance of evil, my spiritual vitality increases (1 Thessalonians 5:22).

Today, some twenty years later, I continue to benefit from the truth learned from my doctoral degree experience. I possessed spiritual vitality when I planned for unforeseen circumstances. (I was already meditating on Jeremiah 17:7-8.) I acquired adequate provisions for my needs rather than living from crisis to crisis. (I had already collected and organized my study materials.) Along with physical and academic provisions, I knew the value of being spiritually prepared. Similar to saving a percentage of each check for unforeseen expenses, I built a spiritual reserve for challenging times. My "terminal degree experience" taught me that the heat would come; the drought is certain; however, there is a supernatural source of vitality when one is spiritually prepared.

As you move into the momentum of *Precious in His Sight,* may I encourage you to choose to cultivate spiritual vitality. Consider implementing this spiritual health plan:

- Exercise your flabby prayer muscles by praying expectantly (John 14:13).
- Refrain from ingesting unnecessary "thought calories" by declining anxious thoughts (Philippians 4:6-7).
- Choose a diet of "high potency thought nutrients," which promotes thoughts that are pleasing, morally clean, and in harmony with God's standards of holiness (Philippians 4:8-9).
- Increase your physical stamina by choosing to rejoice in all circumstances (Nehemiah 8:10; Philippians 4:4; 1 Thessalonians 5:16).
- Cast off unnecessary weight by placing all your concerns on the Lord (1 Peter. 5:7).
- Accept that you are only capable of cultivating spiritual vitality when you seek supernatural assistance (Philippians 4:19).

If you consistently follow this plan you should possess a more finely toned spiritual constitution that allows you to say, "I possess spiritual VITALITY because I choose to:

- be a Victor rather than a victim (Romans 8:26-39),
- walk in Integrity (Psalm 15),
- Trust in the Lord (Proverbs 3:5-6),
- Abide in Christ (John 15:1-11),
- Love my Lord with all my heart (Matthew 22:27-39),
- Incline my heart to my heavenly Father's testimonies (Psalm 119:36),
- Thank my heavenly Father for the benefits of being His child (Psalm 103), and
- Yield myself to the Lord (2 Chronicles 30:8)."

Developing a Gentle and Quiet Spirit

Scriptures to Study

Psalm 1; Jeremiah 17:7-8

For Meditation

Jeremiah 17:7-8

For Further Study

- Study Psalm 1 carefully. Compare the happiness of the righteous person with the painful end of the ungodly person. How will Psalm 1 affect your choices?

- Develop a personal spiritual vitality plan to prepare for unforeseen circumstances.

- Consider Naaman's wife's maid, who clung to her faith despite adverse circumstances (2 Kings 5:1-19). What practical strategies will you develop to help you maintain spiritual vitality in the midst of unforeseen circumstances?

- Using the example at the conclusion of this chapter as a model, develop your own VITALITY acrostic. Support each statement with Scripture.

A Principle to Ponder

Precious in His sight is the woman who, regardless of the circumstances, exhibits spiritual vitality (Jeremiah 17:7-8).

4

Precious in His Sight is...
The Woman Who Joyfully Uses Her Spiritual Gifts

*W*hat would your response be if you carefully selected a gift and presented it to someone dear only to have him or her leave it wrapped? Myriad emotions undoubtedly flood your mind as you consider such an ungrateful response on the part of the recipient. Putting the question in the context of spiritual gifts, is there a possibility that you might be neglecting to unwrap the ones our Lord graciously custom selected for you? Let's identify some principles that will help in identifying and using your spiritual gifts to glorify their Giver, your heavenly Father.

Principle One—The word gift is derived from the Greek word charisma, which emphasizes the freeness of the gift. Your spiritual gifts cannot be earned, pursued, or worked for; all gifts are graciously given by your heavenly Father (1 Corinthians 12:7).

Principle Two—A right understanding of your spiritual gifts should evoke a spirit of humility within you (Romans 12:3).

Principle Three—There is a diversity of unique giftedness that is distributed to enhance the effectiveness of the entire body of believers. God purposely planned these diverse capabilities; He never intended for us to all be the same. In fact, to force uniformity is to run the risk of deformity (Romans 12:4-5).

Principle Four—Your spiritual gifts were graciously given to you; you do not own them but are simply God's steward of them (Romans 12:6; 1 Corinthians 12:4, 7, 11, 18).

Principle Five—You are to align the use of your gifts with your season of life, keeping your biblical priorities in the correct order (Ecclesiastes 3:1-22).

Principle Six—Your spiritual gifts are to be used for the good of the entire body of Christ (1 Corinthians 12:7).

Principle Seven—Spiritual gifts were give to you for the spiritual edification, nurturing, and development of the body. You are to use them to equip others so that they are challenged to move from sin to obedience (Ephesians 4:7-16).

Principle Eight—Spiritual gifts are to be used for the benefit of those in the body, not simply for your exhalation (1 Peter 4:7-11).

Principle Nine—Your heavenly Father will require an accounting of how you used your gifts to further His Kingdom (Matthew 25:14-30).

Principle Ten—There in no excuse for ignorance in the realm of spiritual gifts; you are to be correctly informed about them (1 Corinthians 12:1).

Since the Scriptures challenge us to be correctly informed about the spiritual gifts, let's briefly define several of them:

- Prophecy ministers to others by edifying (building up), exhorting (encouraging), and comforting others in the body of Christ (Romans 12:6; 1 Corinthians 14:1-3; Ephesians 4:11).
- Teaching communicates the Word of God so that others can clearly understand its meaning (Romans 2:17-24; 12:7; Colossians 1:28; 1 Timothy 1:3-7; 4:15-16; 2 Timothy 2:24-26; James 3:1).

3.) • Discernment discriminates between truth and error to stimulate others to function in truth that is motivated by love and provides a foundation for correction in righteousness (Acts 13:6-12; 1 Corinthians 12:10; 2 Timothy 3:16).

4.) • Wisdom provides practical insight into the ways and will of God (1 Samuel 25; Acts 15; 1 Corinthians 12:8-10, 28).

5.) • Knowledge is the ability to acquire and communicate biblical knowledge for the benefit of the church body (Acts 5; 8:26-38; 1 Corinthians 12:8; John 4).

6.) • Leadership motivates, directs, and delegates responsibilities to others; one's personal life is to be an example of the performance expected of others (2 Kings 12:6-8; Nehemiah 2:17-18; Romans 12:8; 1 Thessalonians 5:12-13; Hebrews 13:7).

7.) • Administration understands and facilitates the activities and procedures of others. Different from the gift of leadership, the individual with the gift of administration understands how an organization operates, casts a vision of how to increase its effectiveness, and guides from behind the scenes (2 Kings 12:7-12; 1 Corinthians 12:28; 1 Timothy 3:1-5, 12).

8.) • Exhortation affirms, builds up, and encourage others (Acts 9:26-27; 11:22-23; 13:15; Romans 12:8; 1 Corinthians 4:16, 1 Thessalonians 4:1; 1 Timothy 4:13; 2 Timothy 4:2; 1 Peter 5:1).

9.) • Helps or Service lifts others' burdens by extending a helping hand and creates an environment that allows others to succeed in their areas of giftedness (Acts 6:1-6; Acts 9:36-39; Romans 12:7; Philippians 2:25-30; 1 Peter 4:11).

10.) • Giving uses financial and material resources to further God's work and contributes generously, with a cheerful spirit, and without second thoughts or regrets (Romans 12:8; 2 Corinthians 9:7-14).

- Mercy bestows empathy and seeks to ease the pain and meet the needs of others (Matthew 23:23; Romans 12:8; Titus 3:5; James 3:17).

- Faith is the ability to trust God to do what He says He will do. Such faith is the result of much prayer, is accompanied by the assurance that God is working on one's behalf, and believes God can and will do what others deem impossible (Acts 6:5-8; 11:24; Romans 12:3-6; 1 Corinthians 12:9; Hebrews 11:1).

~~What is the benefit of prayerfully using your spiritual gifts to their maximum potential? Most often, when you excel, the whole body benefits, and you experience incredible fulfillment—if you are exercising them in a spirit of humility~~ (Romans 12:3). However, if you compare, force, or entertain expectations that are beyond your God-given capabilities, mediocrity, frustration, phoniness, or total defeat is predictable. So relax and enjoy using your spiritual gifts. Ask your heavenly Father to help you cultivate your capabilities and develop your own style. And purpose to appreciate the members of your spiritual family for who they are, even though their outlook or approach may be different from yours. Stop comparing and enjoy being you.

To begin the process, consider spending some time pondering the following Heart Search.

Unwrapping My Spiritual Gift...A Personal Heart Search

- Read the passages of Scripture that describe the spiritual gifts—Romans 12:3-8; 1 Corinthians 12:4-10; Ephesians 4:7-16; 1 Peter 4:7-11.
- Confirm that you are a child of God. You won't be given your spiritual gifts until the salvation transaction is completed—Romans 3:10, 23; 5:12; 6:23; 5:8.
- Pray for openness to the leading of the Holy Spirit in relation to the use of your gift—Romans 8:26.

- Examine your desire in the use of your spiritual gifts—Philippians 2:13; Psalm 37:4.
- Identify the needs of your church—1 Corinthians 12:12-27.
- Evaluate your previous ministry-related experiences.
- Listen to the counsel of mature believers—Proverbs 1:5.
- Identify one thing you are involved in that is forcing you to be something you're not. If possible, remove yourself from that activity and see if you sense relief
- What happens when you compare yourself with others? Do you find that you don't match up? Do the results of the comparison give Satan an opportunity to discourage you?
- Are you trying to be something that simply is not you and never will be? Are you willing to accept that your spiritual gifts are different and focus on maximizing them to their utmost?
- Analyze your friendships and determine if you're pressuring someone to conform to your standards or skills. If so, are you willing to back off, let your friend be the person God made him or her to be, and encourage your friend to reach his or her full potential?
- Tell your heavenly Father that you desire to be a faithful steward of the gifts He gave you—Matthew 25:14-30; 1 Peter 4:10.
- Remember that heart searching is profitable; however, one caution is offered. Concentrating too much on yourself can lead to discouragement. Rather, focus on the One who is sufficient for your every need—Philippians 4:19.

Developing a Gentle and Quiet Spirit

Scriptures to Study

> Romans 12:3-8; 1 Corinthians 12:4-10; Ephesians 4:7-16;
> 1 Peter 4:7-11.

For Meditation

> 1 Peter 4:10

For Further Study

- Expand your understanding of spiritual gifts. Use the list, definitions, and suggested scriptural references contained in this chapter as a foundation for your study.

- Align your education, life experiences, talents, and abilities with the spiritual gifts definitions; use specific examples, such as "I enjoy teaching others." Which spiritual gifts match the examples listed? These are undoubtedly some of your spiritual gifts.

- How does your life reflect that you are a good steward of your spiritual gifts (1 Peter 4:10)? Prayerfully ask your heavenly Father if there are any modifications that need to be made to your lifestyle to improve your stewardship. Record your goals and ask someone to hold you accountable for implementing them.

- Study Miriam, whose life reflects both the use and misuse of her spiritual gifts (Exodus 15:19-21; Numbers 12:1-15; 20:1). (See also Matthew 23:23; Romans 12:8; Titus 3:5; James 3:17.)

A Principle to Ponder

> Precious in His sight is the woman who adjusts the use of her spiritual gifts to her season of life (Ecclesiastes 3:1-22).

5

Precious in His Sight is...

The Woman Who is Willing to be Stretched to Communicate God's Message of Hope to Others

The California sun cast a golden glow on the church parking lot as I returned to my car following the morning service. A relatively new member, I was seeking my heavenly Father's wisdom for how I might share my spiritual gifts with this body. My progress was halted when the women's ministry council leader emerged from her car with a question. "Pat, would you be available to teach a chapter from Ephesians for our summer ladies' Bible study?"

I was delighted to be asked, and having already prepared content for one of my classes from chapter four, I suggested that perhaps that would be an appropriate one for me to pray about presenting. Her gracious response was, "Actually, the only chapter remaining is three. Would you be interested in teaching it?"

I asked if I might have some time to pray and review the chapter. She responded positively and indicated that she would have the coordinator of the Bible study contact me.

As we concluded our conversation, I knew that if my heavenly Father wanted me to take this assignment, it would not only be a stretch for me, but I would be spending much time in prayer and preparation. My first responsibility for the afternoon was to prayerfully read Ephesians 3.

My heavenly Father's response was yes, and thus began the treasure hunt to unearth The Secret Plan of God contained in Ephesians Chapter 3.[6] I organized and categorized my findings under four Cs:

- *Context*—understanding how chapter 3 fits into the book of Ephesians
- *Content*—key thoughts from the chapter
- *Connection*—How does Ephesians 3 affect my life?
- *Commitment*—What will I do with what I learned?

Developing the four Cs meant that I needed to read the chapter in the context of the entire book of Ephesians, thus yielding the first C— Context. I learned that the gospel was likely first brought to Ephesus by Aquila and Priscilla, who were left there by Paul on his second missionary journey (Acts 18:18-19, 26). Chapters one through three are theological and emphasize New Testament doctrine; chapters four through six are practical and focus on Christian behavior. Chapter 3 is placed in the instructions of God's purpose for the church (1:3-3:13) and concludes with God's fullness for the church (3:14-21).

As I became immersed in the theology of the first three chapters, I realized that I needed to refocus my thinking about the book's content. Ephesians is not simply a theological book written to impart doctrine and behavior to the church. It was written by Paul, who firmly established the church on his third missionary journey (described in Acts 19). Paul loved the people he had pastored for three years and wrote to them to maintain their relationship, much as we seek to maintain contact when absent from those we love. It is a letter of both encouragement and admonition, written to remind his spiritual children of their immeasurable blessings in Jesus Christ, to encourage them to be thankful for blessings, and to challenge them to live in a manner worthy of their spiritual heritage.

My study then took me to the second C—Content, and I began to identify key thoughts from the chapter. Paul begins this portion of his letter by stating, "For this reason..." This statement introduces the purpose of Paul's prayer, which he actually begins in 2:14. As with all biblical analysis, I had to look back to the truths he presented in chapter 2 to understand the purpose of the prayer (2:11-14). A study of the passage revealed that:

- When a person becomes a Christian, he/she is no longer Jew or Gentile (2:15).
- All believers are in one body (2:16).
- The Gentiles who were once far away become near when they believed (2:17).
- All believers are equal citizens of God's kingdom and members of His family (2:19).
- All believers are being built into God's temple and dwelling (2:21-22).[7]

Paul begins his prayer for believers with the plea that they understand their resources as one in Christ. It seems he then decided to reemphasize some of the truths already mentioned, thus making 3:2-13 a large parenthesis. Perhaps Paul discerned that his spiritual children were not ready to hear his prayer on their behalf until they better understood—and were therefore willing to apply—the truths he was about to pray about. Paul perceived a need to affirm his authority for teaching such a new and far-reaching truth as the oneness of Jew and Gentile in Christ, which he does by saying that God Himself gave him the truth and the commission to proclaim it (3:2-7).

I learned that this parenthesis focuses primarily on the great mystery revealed by God. I needed to reeducate myself about the definition of *mystery*, since it bears no resemblance to our current literary "whodunit." From a biblical perspective, a mystery is a divine secret—something God had not previously revealed but was now ready to unveil. And what is the great mystery revealed by God? Gentiles and Jews are one in Christ and there is no longer any distinction.

In Ephesians 1:1-3:13 Paul gives the basic truths about the Christian life—who we are in Christ and the great unlimited resources we have in Him. In 3:14-21 he exhorts us to claim and to live by those truths, while in 3:14-21 Paul gives his prayer requests on behalf of the Ephesian believers. In his first prayer, Paul urges them to live in the full power and effectiveness of "every spiritual blessing in the heavenly places" in Christ (1:3; see also 15-23). He wants his spiritual children to know their power. I need to comprehend that power as well.

His second prayer is for enablement—for them to use their power. Paul calls on God to activate believers' power so that they will become faithful children and thereby glorify their heavenly Father. He prays specifically for:

- the inner strength of the Spirit (Ephesians 3:14-16)
- the indwelling of Christ in the believer's heart (Ephesians 3: 17a)
- incomprehensible love to permeate their lives (Ephesians 3:17b-19a)
- them to have God's own fullness (Ephesians 3:3:19b)
- God's glory thereby to be manifested and proclaimed (Ephesians 3:20-21)

As I focused on Ephesians 3:20-21, I was reminded of the little book *My Heart Christ's Home*,[8] which provides a graphic picture of the message Paul is communicating to his spiritual children. In this booklet Boyd Munger pictures the Christian life as a house, through which Jesus goes from room to room. Only when He has cleaned every room, closet, and corner from sin and foolishness can He settle down and be at home. The message of *My Heart Christ's Home* prompted the third C—Connection, as I asked myself, *how does Ephesians 3 affect my life?* My mind formed several questions:

- Am I willing to allow my Lord to clean every room, closet, and corner of sin and foolishness so He can settle down and be at home in my life?

- Do the lives of Aquila and Priscilla (Acts 18:18-19, 26), who provide role models for the use of spiritual gifts for both men and women in the local church, challenge me to use my spiritual gifts in my local church?
- Am I willing to have spiritual truth reinforced in my life? Paul's letter to his spiritual children reinforces the need for repetition when learning biblical truth. It reminds me that I should not be discouraged if I do not understand everything about a truth when I first hear it, nor should I chafe if I need further instruction.
- In this portion of Paul's letter to the Ephesians, he challenges his children to apply what they know. Am I theologically sound but practically inept? Am I a doer of the Word or simply a hearer (James 1:21-25)?

Sincerely desiring to have an affirmative response to these questions prompted the fourth C—Commitment. What will I do with what I have learned? I began by focusing on one concept that I believed my Lord would have me apply to my life. My heart was drawn to Ephesians 3:20, for I realized that if I meet the conditions of verses 16-19, God's power working in and through me is unlimited and far beyond my comprehension.[9]

As I taught the Bible study, I gave each lady a card and challenged her to write out one concept that she believed the Lord would have her apply to her life from Ephesians 3, to daily record progress toward its application on the card, and to consistently review her heavenly Father's work in her life.

Once the teaching of the Bible study was completed, I reflected on the series of events that began in the church parking lot and concluded with the priceless privilege of communicating God's Word. Most assuredly, I had spent much time in preparation and prayer; however, through each phase of the preparation and delivery my heavenly Father guided, directed, and encouraged me. Had I been unwilling to be stretched, I would have bypassed an incredible opportunity to use my spiritual gifts.

As you are confronted with stretching experiences, may I challenge you to prayerfully consider accepting them? If you will approach them believing that you can "do all things through Christ who strengthens [you]" (Philippians 4:13 NKJV), you will undoubtedly experience the reality of Ephesians 3:20 in your life.

Developing a Gentle and Quiet Spirit

Scriptures to Study

Acts 18:18-19, 26; Ephesians 3

For Meditation

Ephesians 3:20-21

For Further Study

- Spend some time studying the great mystery revealed by God in Ephesians 2:3-13. Focus on the five aspects of the great mystery: the prisoner of the mystery—Ephesians 3:1-4, the plan of the mystery—Ephesians 3:5-6, the preaching of the mystery—Ephesians 3:7-9, the purpose of the mystery—Ephesians 3:10-11, and the privilege of the mystery—Ephesians 3:12-13.

- Write down specific examples that can help you define whether you are theologically sound or practically inept. Are you a doer of the Word or simply a hearer (James 1:21-25)? Evaluate Matthew 7:21-27 in light of your response.

- What evidence can you cite in your life that reflects that your heavenly Father has allowed you to accomplish work that far exceeded what you thought you could do (Ephesians 3:20-21)? Write out a prayer that expresses your gratitude to Him.

- What can you learn from Priscilla (Acts 18:18-19, 26), who, along with her husband, Aquila, provides a role model for the use of spiritual gifts for both men and women in the local church?

A Principle to Ponder

Precious in His sight is the woman who is both theologically sound and practically adept (James 1:21-25).

6

Precious in His Sight is...

The Woman Who Wears Garments That Reflect Her Royal Heritage

When the first day of spring arrives and you anticipate warmer days, your fashion choices shift to cooler colors and lighter-weight fabrics. While lightening the color depth and fabric weight, the fashion industry at the same time tends to minimize the amount of fabric that spring garments contain. As a woman who desires to please your heavenly Father, you have the challenge of selecting clothing that reflects His instructions to adorn yourself modestly and discreetly (1 Timothy 2:9-10). So you are faced with a dilemma: Will you choose modesty or fashion? If you wholeheartedly embrace biblical standards of modesty, must you eliminate from your wardrobe anything fashionable? Let's take a look at what Scripture teaches.

Modesty is a word that is not heard very often anymore—and when you do hear it, it is often classified as a practice applicable to the Victorian era. By definition *modesty* means "having or showing regard for the decencies of behavior, speech and dress."[10] Spiritually, modesty is an issue of the heart. If your thoughts are focused on the attributes found in Philippians 4:8-9, more than likely your external appearance will be modest.

Many believe that the modesty standards described in the Scriptures are obsolete rather than an absolute standard that twenty-first-century Christian women are challenged to embrace. However, the immutability (changelessness) of God would be in question if the Scriptures that provide you with a standard for dress are not timelessly relevant. If you think that God changed His mind about one passage of Scripture, how can you be sure that He has not changed His mind about others? Let's look at several Scriptures that can guide your clothing choices:

- *Deuteronomy 22:5*—Your clothing should be feminine, and others should be able to discern that you are a woman.
- *Proverbs 31:21-25*—Your clothing should reflect quality workmanship.
- *Romans 12:1-2*—You are "in" the world but not "of" the world. A mature believer has developed the ability to separate herself from an ungodly society, including the area of clothing selection when it is contrary to biblical principles. Current trends in fashion are not the final authority in what is acceptable for us to wear as believers.
- *1 Timothy 2:9-10*—Your clothing is to be modest, with propriety (what is proper) and moderation (a command for Christian women). This can be applied to the style of our clothes as well as the quantity of clothes we have; both should reflect the principle of modesty.[11]

Throughout Scripture there are examples of aesthetically pleasing clothing for both men and women.

- The garments for the priests were constructed by skilled artisans (Exodus 31:10; 35:19).
- The children of Israel were instructed to attach blue tassels on their garments to remind them of their need to trust and obey God's commands (Numbers 15:37-38).[12]

- The wise woman of Proverbs 31 wore garments of fine linen and purple (Proverbs 31:22).
- The people of Zion were challenged to "awake" and put on "beautiful garments" (Isaiah 52:1).
- One of our Lord's garments was woven without seams (John 23-24).
- The attire for the marriage supper of the Lamb is fine linen (Revelation 19:8).

As you study these Scriptures I believe you will be able to say with confidence that for godly women, modesty is an absolute value for the twenty-first century.

So, must you look dowdy to be godly? Dowdy is an adjective that compresses into one word a description of everything that lacks style and color, is out of date, and looks shabby. As you study 1 Peter 3:3-5, you will find that Peter is not suggesting that women assume a dowdy appearance. However, in Peter's day, as in ours, women put heavy emphasis on their appearance. He is not trying to say women should not dress attractively. He is saying that they should not concentrate on making appearance their sole source of beauty (1 Peter 3:3).

His illustration of lasting beauty refers the reader to the holy women who did not adorn themselves with the temporal cultural extravagances of their day, but rather with the timeless hope in God that produces beauty of character and disposition (1 Peter 3:4-5). Sarah (1 Peter 3:6) is cited as an example of a woman who possessed inner beauty, character, and modesty (Genesis 12:11-20; Hebrews 11:11).

Peter is also encouraging women to refrain from being extreme—to dress attractively, but to use discretion and dress modestly. His challenge is that their beauty should not simply be a matter of outward appearance.

Solomon's counsel captures the thought in seventeen words: "Like a gold ring in a pig's snout is a beautiful woman without discretion" (Proverbs 11:22).

Let's focus on some tips for dressing that make 1 Peter 3:3 practical:

- Your face displays your character. Proverbs 15:13 (NASB) teaches us that a "joyful heart makes a cheerful face." You can draw attention to your face by selecting necklines that complement it. For example, a collar or bow allows the eye to linger on the face.

- Test your garments for wearability. Do this by positioning yourself in front of a mirror to observe what others will see.

  Bend over to check how revealing your neckline is.
  Sit down and cross your legs to check the length of shorts and skirts.
  Bend over to see how far your skirt moves up.
  Take a large step to examine skirt slits.
  Place your hands above your head to see how much of the midriff is exposed.

- Take the "Truth in Packaging Inventory."

  Your clothing is a label for your character. What does it communicate about you?
  What values determine the clothing you wear?
  When you select your clothing, what are your first thoughts?
  When you dress for the day, who are you thinking about pleasing?
  What is your response to the question "Is modesty an absolute or obsolete value for the twenty-first-century Christian woman?"

Customs of dress change with the seasons, and fashions are as fickle as the wind. Any woman who puts her hopes in these to make herself look beautiful will find her standards of beauty constantly changing. Precious in His sight is the woman who directs her energy on her character first and her physical appearance second. This woman will ensure that her beauty will last.

Developing a Gentle and Quiet Spirit

Scriptures to Study

> Deuteronomy 22:5; Proverbs 11:22; 31:21-25; Romans 12:1-2;
> 1 Timothy 2:9-10; 1 Peter 2:21-3:22

For Meditation

> 1 Peter 3:3

For Further Study

- Use the "Truth in Packaging Inventory" to evaluate your grooming practices. Record any changes that need to be made to allow your outward and inward beauty to complement each other. Develop a strategy to implement the changes.
- Use the Scriptures presented in this chapter to respond to the question "If I wholeheartedly embrace biblical standards of modesty, must I eliminate from my wardrobe anything fashionable?"
- Study the life of Sarah, a woman who possessed inner and external beauty, character, and modesty (Genesis 12:11-20; Hebrews 11:11; 1 Peter 3:6).

A Principle to Ponder

> Precious in His sight is the woman who acknowledges that God's brand of modesty is always in style (1 Timothy 1:9).

7

Precious in His Sight is...

The Woman Who Understands Singleness From Her Heavenly Father's Perspective

As a Christian woman trained as a home economist, I never expected to be single past my mid-twenties. However, the Lord had a different plan for me. He has gently matured my attitude toward singleness. I know now that the purpose of marriage is not only to provide an intimate, nurturing relationship between two people. I should marry only if our united lives would be more effective for the Lord than either of us is in our single state.

good point!

I established Home Economics departments in two Christian colleges, and I have had the joy of watching numerous young women mature into useful instruments for our Master's kingdom. Though I have no children of my own, I have spiritual children and grandchildren all over the world. My single status allows me to provide the nurturing that my students need without neglecting my own family. I daily have the joy of practicing what Paul wrote about in 1 Corinthians 7:32-34.

My greatest challenge in experiencing contentment in my single state is when I encounter members of the body of Christ who cannot understand how someone who can cook and sew, as well as implement effective management and financial skills, is not married. Their insistence that "Mr. Right" will one day come along discounts the possibility that it is the Lord's will for me to minister to others as a single person, using my unique spiritual gifts, talents, and educational background.[13]

Current statistics remind us that "overall, there are significantly more unmarried women than men: 89 single men for every 100 single women."[14] This imbalance suggests that a significant percentage of Christian women will not marry.

Paul addresses the practical advantages of singleness in 1 Corinthians 7:7-9 and 25-40. One primary reason for remaining single, according to Paul, is the special freedom and independence afforded to the individual.

It is important that the Christian community encourage a single woman toward spiritual maturity so that she is prepared for her heavenly Father's next assignment (Jeremiah 29:11-13). For the single woman, spiritual maturity includes growing in her personal character (Proverbs 31:30), understanding God's purpose for the home (Genesis 2:21-24), developing a heart of contentment (John 14:1-3), learning how to effectively manage her current home (Proverbs 24:3), growing in graciousness (Proverbs 11:16), practicing biblical stewardship (Philippians 4:11-12), implementing hospitality (Romans 12:13), broadening her world view (Matthew 5:13-16), understanding the contribution she can make to the body of Christ (Romans 12:4-6), and embracing the truth of Titus 2:3-5 so that God's Word is not discredited. The following table offers some suggestions for the body of Christ to assist the single woman in achieving her completeness in Christ (Colossians 3:10).

Precious In His Sight Is The Single Woman Who:	
PRINCIPLE	ACCOMPLISHED BY
Focuses her time and energy on her character development (Ruth 3:11)	Learning from the wisdom of others (Proverbs 1:7) Embracing the eleven principles of the wise woman virtuous, trustworthy, energetic, physically fit, economical, unselfish, honorable, lovable, prepared and God fearing (Proverbs 31:10-31)[15]
Acknowledges the strategic position of the home (Genesis 2:21-24)	Studying the culture of the twenty-first century in light of the Scriptures (2 Timothy 3:1-17) Seeking to be a faithful steward of every relationship (1 Corinthians 4:1-2)
Develops a heart of contentment (John 14:1-3)	Maintaining a diligent heart (Proverbs 4:23) Choosing forgiveness and flexibility (1 Peter 5:5-6)
Manages her home prudently (Proverbs 24:3)	Faithfully maintaining her current living environment (Proverbs 31:27) Implementing effective methods of household management (Colossians 3:23)
Chooses to grow in graciousness (Proverbs 11:16)	Abiding by standard etiquette protocol (Proverbs 11:22) Displaying gratitude (1 Thessalonians 5:18)
Practices biblical stewardship (Matthew 25:21)	Understanding and applying basic budgeting principles (Proverbs 27:23-24) Choosing to learn and implement time management strategies (Psalm 90:12)
Implements hospitality (Romans 12:13)	Developing a scriptural attitude toward hospitality (Hebrews 13:2) Focusing on being the hostess rather than the guest (1 Peter 4:9)
Develops a biblical world view (Matthew 5:13-16)	Purposing to broaden her world (Luke 2:52) Casting her vision beyond her own needs to the needs of others (John 4:34-38)
Accepts her unique position in the body of Christ (Romans 12:4-13)	Thriving in her single state (1 Corinthians 7:7-9; 25-40) Meditating on the fact that God loves her (Philippians 4:8-9)
Practices the Titus 2 principle (Titus 2:3-5)	Willingly practicing the Titus 2:3-5 instruction (1 Samuel 15:22). Being as excited about being a mentor as having one (Luke 6:38).

A single woman who seeks to be Precious in His sight, as well as those in the body of Christ who desire to nurture the single woman, must understand that marriage is not a condition for salvation, a command, or the standard for everyone. Reflecting on 1 Corinthians 7:17-24, she is encouraged to be content with her marital status and wholeheartedly serve her Lord rather than living in a state of limbo until "Mr. Right" appears (1 Corinthians 7:32; Philippians 4:11; Hebrews 13:5).

The teachings of Jesus in Matthew 19:12 suggest that He believed singleness is a good thing. As we study the Scriptures we find a number of single individuals who positively impacted our Father's kingdom, including the apostle Paul, Lazarus, Mary, Martha, and the Lord Jesus Himself. If singleness were an acceptable state for the Son of God, how can we reject it?

*contentment is key, not where my marital status is.

Developing a Gentle and Quiet Spirit

Scriptures to Study

>Psalm 37:3-4; Proverbs 3:5-6; Jeremiah 29:11-13;
>1 Corinthians 7:1-10, 32-34

For Meditation

>Psalm 84:11

For Further Study

- What do the "Scriptures to Study" listed above teach you about learning to be content in the state you are currently in (Philippians 4:13)?
- Using Psalm 103 as your format, craft a prayer to your heavenly Father, thanking Him for the state you are currently in. Be specific, just as the psalmist was. Meditate on the prayer daily for a week. At its conclusion, evaluate your level of contentment.
- What specific ways can you be an encouragement to a single woman? Select one way and implement it this week.
- Evaluate the character of Dorcas, a widow, who was affirmed for her good works and acts of charity (Acts 9:32-42).

A Principle to Ponder

>Precious in His sight is the woman who uses her days of singleness to concentrate on becoming complete in Christ (Colossians 3:10).

Precious in His Sight is...

The Woman Who Models Her Heavenly Father's Character

[handwritten margin note: imitator is used in the Bible only 6 times in the context of God. only one time to be an imitator of what is not good. It says you are to be like a mimic. you do what you imitate]

*E*phesians 5:1 challenges believers to "be <u>imitators</u> of God, as beloved children." Writing on this verse, John MacArthur states, *[handwritten margin note: great quote]* "The Christian has no greater calling or purpose than that of imitating his Lord. That is the very purpose of sanctification, growing in likeness to the Lord while serving Him on earth. The Christian life is designed to reproduce godliness as modeled by the Savior and Lord, Jesus Christ, in whose image believers have been recreated through the new birth. As God's dear children, believers are to become more and more like their heavenly Father."[16] Since Scripture is adamant in its instructions to model our heavenly Father's character, spending time analyzing it is a worthwhile study. Both Psalm 86 and Psalm 145 provide us with a synopsis of His character. Let's focus on Psalm 145 and evaluate it from two perspectives. The first is to identify the character of our heavenly Father; secondly, the findings are placed in practical terms by asking, "How am I to model His character?"

The chart that follows summarizes the analysis. Let me encourage you to take the time to read each of the Scriptures in the application column and allow them to challenge you to emulate your heavenly Father.

What Is My Heavenly Father Like?		How Am I To Model His Character?
VERSE	QUALITY	APPLICATION
1	Worthy of praise	Recall that the Psalms are directed to the will and not the emotions; therefore, I will offer praise at all times (Psalms 34:1, 103, 104). A great project is to read through the Psalms and underline each time the psalmist says, "I will . . ."
2	Deserving of continual praise	Purpose to praise God throughout the day (Psalm 50:23; Ephesians 5:20; 1 Thessalonians 5:18)
3	Great. This means "first-rate, excellent, notable, remarkable, highly significant, and distinguished."[17]	Choose to be a servant (Matthew 20:26; 23:11; Mark 10:43; John 13:1-16—an example; 1 Corinthians 9:19-22)
8	Gracious	Purpose to integrate the attributes of graciousness—benevolence, kindness, and courtesy—so that my behavior brings honor to my heavenly Father (Proverbs 11:16)
8	Merciful	Demonstrate kindness in excess of what might be expected or demanded by fairness (Luke 6:27-38) and a disposition to forgive (Matthew 6:14-15; John 13:15)
8	Full of compassion	Express sorrow for the sufferings or troubles of others, with the urge to help (Matthew 6:36-38; 20:29-34; Luke 10:29-38)
8	Slow to anger	Be quick to acknowledge that anger generated by selfishness and pride is a sin (5:22) and purpose to resolve conflict as rapidly as possible (Romans 12:17-21; Ephesians 4:262-27; James 5:16)
9	Good to all	Be ready to offer assistance to others, being careful not to discriminate among persons in any way (Proverbs 31:20; James 2:1-4)
9	His tender mercies are over all His works	Realize that whatever I do is to be aligned with the character of my Lord and completed in a manner that reflects the quality of His workmanship (1 Corinthians 10:31; Colossians 3:17)

What Is My Heavenly Father Like?		How Am I To Model His Character?
VERSE	**QUALITY**	**APPLICATION**
10-12	All His works praise Him	Live in such a way that those closest to me affirm my character (Ruth 2:8-12; 3:10-11; Proverbs 31:28-29; 1 Timothy 2:14)
13	His kingdom is an everlasting kingdom; His dominion endures through all generations	Purpose to leave a godly heritage for future generations, remembering that there is no aspect of a human being's life that is not drastically affected by the family from which he/she comes (Psalm 79:13; 1 Timothy 4:6; 2 Timothy 1:3-5)
14	Upholds all who fall; raises up all those who are bowed down	Be an encouragement to those who fall, remembering that if we rejoice at the misfortune of others, we are identifying ourselves as their enemies (Psalms 34:19-22; 37:23-24; Proverbs 24:16; Micah 7:8)
15	Provider	Be ready to give of myself (Luke 6:38; 1 Timothy 5:8; 1 Peter 3:15)
16	Satisfies the desire of every living thing	Develop trust in my heavenly Father as a natural source for my every need (Proverbs 3:5-6; Matthew 6:8; Luke 12:29-31; Philippians 4:6-7, 19)
17	Righteous in all His ways, holy in all His works, and kind in all His deeds	Do my work in such a way that my heavenly Father is glorified (Proverbs 31:23, 31; Ecclesiastes 9:10; Matthew 5:14-16; Colossians 3:17, 23-4)
18	Near to all who call upon Him in truth	Be available to those with legitimate needs—love in deed and in truth (James 2:14-21; 1 John 3:18)
19	Fulfills the desires of those who fear Him	Focus on the reality that to fear God I must possess a reverential trust in Him, including the hatred of evil, and that to acquire spiritual knowledge and wisdom I must first embrace this reverential trust (Job 28:28; Proverbs 1:7, 20-33; 3:7; 8:13; 9:10; 14:26-27)

What Is My Heavenly Father Like?		How Am I To Model His Character?
VERSE	QUALITY	APPLICATION
20	Preserves (keeps) all those who love Him	Take care of those He has placed under my care (Proverbs 31:15, 27; 2 Corinthians 12:14; 1 Timothy 5:3-5; Titus 2:3-5)
	Destroys the wicked	Allow God to straighten the record when the wicked treat me unjustly (Psalms 31:23; 94:12-15; Proverbs 11:5; Isaiah 13:11; Nahum 1:3; 2 Thessalonians 1:3-10; Revelation 20:11-15).
21	Worthy of praise	Intentionally plan my words so that my lips speak the praise of the Lord (Psalms 19:14; 34:1; 42:5, 11; 50:23; 63:3; 71:14-15; Matthew 12:31-37; Luke 6:45)
21	Worthy to be blessed eternally	Behave in a way that reflects I am a daughter of the King (Proverbs 31:30-31; Matthew 5:14-16; Romans 12:1-2; Ephesians 5:1; 1 Peter 1:13-16)

Identifying the character of your heavenly Father is a life-long endeavor—as is the assimilation process. Though you will never completely fulfill the goal, your challenge is to embrace the single purpose of the apostle Paul: "I press on toward the goal for the prize of the upward call of God in Christ Jesus" (Philippians 3:13-14). Precious in His sight is the woman who accepts the challenge, realizes she can only fulfill it through the strength of her heavenly Father (Philippians 4:19), and anticipates, with joy, His affirmation (Matthew 5:21; 2 Timothy 4:6-8).

Developing a Gentle and Quiet Spirit

Scriptures to Study

Psalms 86, 145; Matthew 5:48; 1 Peter 1:15-16

For Meditation

Ephesians 5:1

For Further Study

* Use Psalm 86, and the format used to analyze Psalm 145 in this chapter, to respond to the questions "What is my heavenly Father like?" and "How am I to model His character?"

* What steps will you take to embrace the single purpose of the apostle Paul found in Philippians 3:13-14?

* Evaluate Eve, the only perfect woman ever created. Focus on the positive attributes of her character (Genesis 1:27-28; 2:18, 20-25; 3:1-20)

A Principle to Ponder

Precious in His sight is the woman who seeks to model her heavenly Father's character (Matthew 5:48; Ephesians 5:1; 1 Peter 1:15-16).

9

Precious in His Sight is...

The Woman Who Chooses to Evaluate Her Spiritual Growth

*A*s you progressed through this section of *Precious in His Sight,* you spent time in your heavenly Father's company, cultivating character qualities that contributed to the development of a gentle and quiet spirit. If you chose to allow the unchanging Word of God to be consistently applied to your life, when faced with life's challenges you became a victor rather than a victim. It is now time to evaluate the impact of this section and to project growth for the sections that follow. I invite you to prayerfully consider the following questions and respond by recording your current status in the pursuit of the cultivation of a gentle and quiet spirit.

Do I...
- filter my daily decisions through the changeless instructions found in God's Word (Psalm 119:9-16)?
- allow the testing of my faith to produce deeper communion and greater trust in Christ, or do I waste the test (James 1:2-5)?
- choose to exhibit spiritual vitality regardless of the circumstances (Jeremiah 17:7-8)?

- desire to be a faithful steward of the gifts my heavenly Father gave me (Matthew 25:14-30; 1 Peter 4:10)?
- approach stretching experiences believing that I can "do all things through Christ who strengthens me" (Philippians 4:13)?
- have priorities that reflect an eternal perspective and follow the model of the Lord Jesus, who glorified His Father while on earth while finishing the work He gave Him to do (John 17:4)?
- deliberately bring thoughts of little or big needs to Christ's control (2 Corinthians 10:5)?
- seek to fulfill "the royal law according to the Scripture," (James 2:8) and love my neighbor as myself (Matthew 22:37-40)?
- use Scripture to replace my fear of man with the knowledge that God is sufficient to override my fears (Psalm 56:3, 11)?
- acknowledge that God's brand of modesty is always in style (1 Timothy 1:9)?
- use my days of singleness to concentrate on becoming complete in Christ (Colossians 3:10)?
- base my sense of worth on the unchanging standard of God's Word rather than the propaganda of the world (Isaiah 43:21; 2 Corinthians 4:7)?
- purpose to forgive even when I am maligned, neglected, and unappreciated (Luke 23:34)?'
- purpose to be an imitator of God (Matthew 5:48; Ephesians 5:1; 1 Peter 1:15-16)?

Developing a Gentle and Quiet Spirit

Scriptures to Study

> Ephesians 4:1-3; Philippians 1:6; 3:13; 4:6-9

For Meditation

> 1 Corinthians 11:31

For Further Study

- Prayerfully craft specific goals that will motivate your growth toward the continued development of a gentle and quiet spirit.
- Review the life of Rahab. She allowed God to polish her marred reputation so that at the conclusion of her life, she was worthy to be one of the two women recorded in the gallery of the heroes and heroines of faith (Joshua 2:1-21; 6:22-25; James 2:25; Hebrews 11:30-31)

A Principle to Ponder

> Precious in His sight is the woman who regularly evaluates her spiritual growth (2 Peter 3:18)

The Godly Woman and Her Relationships
Precious in His Sight is the Woman Who:

10

Precious in His Sight is...

The Woman Who Chooses to be a
Grateful Mentee

*A*s mentioned in Chapter One, an intentional spiritual dietary
plan is just as essential to your spiritual growth as a deliberate
food diet plan is fundamental to your physical well-being. If you feel that
a tutor or coach may be needed to help you improve your spiritual and/or
physical nutritional habits, you may wish to pursue a mentor.

Titus 2:3-5 paints a word picture of the character of the mentor.
She is an older woman who possesses the character, knowledge, skills,
expertise, and experience the younger woman desires and the willingness
to offer guidance to assimilate those attributes into her life.[18] The biblical
rationale for mentoring is clearly articulated in Titus 2:5—so "that the
word of God may not be reviled."

Mentoring should flow from one season to another, much like the
seasons and times appointed by God (depicted in Ecclesiastes 3:1-8).
Committed mentors and mentees possess a willingness to remain faithful
to the relationship as it proceeds through the seasons cycle.

The following chart offers some suggestions to assist the mentor and
mentee in establishing guidelines and expectations for each season of
their relationship:

Seasons of the Mentoring Relationship	
SEASON	CHARACTERISTICS
Acquaintance "the older women likewise, that they be reverent in behavior, not slanderers, not given to much wine, teachers of good things." —Titus 2:3 NKJV	The mentor is flexible in her mentoring strategies. She is willing to discuss the expectations of the relationship and how it differs from discipleship. The mentee meets regularly with the mentor to learn how to study the Bible, explore theological issues, pray, and use her spiritual gifts. Mentoring is not to be a dependent relationship but a growing friendship that emerges as time is spent with a woman who possesses the character, knowledge, skills, expertise, and experience the younger woman desires to assimilate into her own life.
Tutoring or Coaching "That they admonish the young women to love their husbands, to love their children, to be discreet, chaste, homemakers, good, obedient to their own husbands." —Titus 2:4-5 NKJV	The women get to know each other, their interests, their goals, and their previous experiences. The women agree to be vulnerable in the relationship.
Counseling and Guidance "That the word of God may not be blasphemed." —Titus 2:5b NKJV	The older woman is to be open, vulnerable, and modeling behavior that reflects her spiritual age. Often the mentoring relationship remains at the season of counseling and guidance.
Friendship "A friend loves at all times." —Proverbs 17:17	Should the mentoring relationship continue, the season of counseling and guidance gently fades into a season of friendship. Just as the difference between the final day of winter and the first day of spring is subtle, so is the transition that marks the disappearance of intergenerational boundaries when the mentoring relationship turns to friendship. Characteristic of the season of friendship is the willingness on the part of both women to share intimately.

Seasons of the Mentoring Relationship	
SEASON	Characteristics
Spiritual Replication "I have no greater joy than this, to hear of my children walking in the truth." —3 John 1:4 NASB	Introduces spiritual children into the mentoring relationship. When a new younger woman desires to be mentored, the original younger woman becomes the mature woman or spiritual mother, while the older woman transitions to the role of spiritual grandmother. The truth of 1 John 1:4 is evident in the lives of both women as the seasons cycle replicates itself. The roles of the women reverse in the season of spiritual replication. The newly mature woman charts the direction and the older woman supports her.

Since this type of relationship may be new for the mentee, it is often helpful for her to be presented with some guidelines for the relationship. The mentoring principles that follow provide a foundation by which a grateful Titus 2 mentee responds to her mentoring relationship:

- Mentoring is a privilege, not a right.
- Your mentor is sharing her most valuable resource with you— her time.
- Sometimes the mentor and mentee will be very similar; other times they will be very different.
- A mentor is someone the younger woman trusts—a mentee is to be found trustworthy.
- The mentee joyfully completes the projects her mentor assigns.
- The mentee remembers that confidentiality is the foundation of a strong mentoring relationship.
- A mentee expects her mentor to ask probing questions that help her discover the "why" behind the challenges that are being faced.
- Biblical mentoring is about character formation.
- The mentoring relationship takes time to develop.

- Mentoring is not meant to be a formal counseling session, but one sister helping another focus and make choices.
- The season of life for both the younger and older woman impacts the style of mentoring.
- The mentoring relationship will not always proceed through the entire seasons cycle.
- Both women consistently communicate their expectations to each other.
- The younger woman is to adjust her schedule to the older woman's.
- Mentoring is to be creative and intentional.
- The mentor and mentee must be willing to allow each other to see their real lives.
- Time and shared experiences move the mentoring relationship through the seasons cycle.
- Confidence, know-how, and healing grow out of healthy relationships when the mentor and the mentee purpose to confess their sins, pray, and trust each other.
- A mature mentor relationship means the women have earned the right to say things that might otherwise seem too personal.
- A maturing mentee consistently expresses her gratitude to her mentor.
- The mentee learns and practices "The Mentee Alphabet."

The Mentee Alphabet

A Mentee...

*A*ccepts her mentor the way she is.

*B*elieves in the counsel and wisdom of her mentor.

*C*alls her mentor just to say, "Hi."

*D*oesn't take advantage of her mentor's graciousness.

*E*nvisions the contribution her mentor will make to her life—
but is realistic.

*F*orgives her mentor's mistakes.

*G*ives to her mentor instead of consistently expecting to receive.

*H*elps her mentor whenever possible.

*I*nvites her mentor to accompany her to non-mentoring activities.

*J*ust wants to spend time with her.

*K*eeps her mentor in her prayers.

*L*oves her mentor for who she is rather than simply the contribution she can make to the mentee's life.

*M*akes an effort to be on time to all scheduled times together.

*N*ever judges.

*O*ffers encouragement to her mentor.

*P*ractices the wisdom and skill her mentor provides.

*Q*uickly expresses gratitude for the contribution the mentor is making to her life.

*R*esponds to her mentor's suggestions.

*S*ays affirming things about her mentor.

*T*ells her mentor the truth.

*U*nderstands her mentor has other responsibilities.

*V*alues the privilege of being mentored.

*W*atches how her mentor interacts with others.

X-plains the "whys" of her behaviors.

*Y*ields her right to be in control.

Adds *Z*est to her mentor's life.

The mentoring relationship provides incredible accountability for both the mentor and mentee, and the fruit of the mentoring relationship will differ for each mentor/mentee combination. However, because of God's faithfulness (Philippians 1:6), both can bequeath a rich heritage to future generations because each chose to obey the biblical mandate of Titus 2:3-5.

Developing a Gentle and Quiet Spirit

Scriptures to Study

    Proverbs 17:17; Luke 1:39-56; 1 Corinthians 4:16; 11:1; Titus 2:3-5; 3 John 1:4

For Meditation

    Philippians 1:3-6

For Further Study

- Study Titus 2:3-5. List some practical ways that an older woman could teach younger women to love their husbands, love their children, be sensible and chaste, be home-lovers, be kindhearted, and be willing to adapt themselves to their husbands.

- Designate several individuals whom you could be a mentor to at your physical and/or spiritual age. Describe how you might foster the relationship. Begin to pursue a relationship today by praying that our heavenly Father will prepare both your heart and that of the potential mentee.

- Elizabeth served as a mentor to Mary. Read Luke 1:39-56. What character qualities did Mary learn from Elizabeth during her three-month residence? (document each with scriptural references.)

- Study the mentor relationship shared by Naomi and Ruth (Ruth 1-3). What lessons can you learn from their lives that are applicable to yours?

- Write to one or more of the women who serve as mentors in your life, thanking them for their impact. Record their names, why you chose them, and the date the note was sent.

A Principle to Ponder

    Precious in His sight is the woman who, as a maturing mentee, consistently expresses her gratitude to her mentor (1 Thessalonians 5:18).

11

Precious in His Sight is...
The Woman Who Embraces Impartiality

As a young professional unfamiliar with the dynamics of the inner workings of college life, I was both amazed and delighted when I received a phone call from the academic vice president's wife. New to the institution herself, her gentle Southern drawl warmly invited me to "come and ride with us" to a function for women of the college. Throughout her years as the "Academic First Lady," Melinda's graciousness and impartiality among our college family, as well as the church that sponsored the institution, provided a unifying force. Even when the dark shadow of divorce fell across the life she knew, her gracious poise and trust in her heavenly Father served as an incredible role model for those who knew her. Because she embraced graciousness and impartiality throughout her tenure, her support group was drawn from a wide assortment of ages, professional standings, and social circles.

Graciousness and impartiality are Siamese twins. Graciousness is blatantly absent in twenty-first-century Christian culture, suggesting that impartiality is most likely missing as well. *Gracious* is defined as "being kindly disposed or showing favor and mercy to someone, usually by a person of superior position and power."[19] Scriptural instances portray

Potiphar dealing graciously with Joseph (Genesis 39:4), Ruth finding favor in the eyes of Boaz (Ruth 2:10), and King Ahasureus's gracious treatment of Esther (Esther 2:17; 5:2).

Our heavenly Father sets the standard for graciousness toward human beings, as stated in the ancient liturgical formula: "The Lord, the Lord, a God merciful and gracious, slow to anger, and abounding in steadfast love and faithfulness" (Exodus 34:6). Psalm 86:15 portrays God as "merciful and gracious, slow to anger and abounding in steadfast love and faithfulness." Psalm 103:8 declares, "The Lord is merciful and gracious, slow to anger and abounding in steadfast love," while Psalm 145:8 affirms, "The Lord is gracious and merciful, slow to anger and abounding in steadfast love."[20]

Impartiality means "not partial or biased."[21] To understand impartiality you must first define *partial*—which, from a biblical perspective, "originally referred to raising someone's face or elevating someone strictly on a superficial, external basis, such as appearance, race, wealth, rank, or social status."[22] James 2:1-17 challenges Christians to shun the sin of partiality (2:9) by focusing on how the Lord Jesus, the King of the universe, chose to make His advent on earth.

- He was born in a stable (Luke 2:7) and possessed a less than impressive genealogy (Matthew 1:1-16).
- He lived in the humble village of Nazareth for thirty years (Matthew 2:19-23; Luke 2:39).
- He selected men engaged in a variety of professions as His disciples (Matthew 18:22; Mark 1:16-20).
- He ministered in Galilee and Samaria, two communities notoriously held in contempt by Israel's leaders (Matthew 1:23-25; John 4).
- He ate with tax collectors and sinners (Matthew 9:10-12).
- He associated with women of questionable reputation (John 4:1-26; 8:1-11).

James compares the church's reaction to the rich and the poor (2:2-4) and concludes that the church is to be a classless society since its primary concern is to fulfill the royal law and "love your neighbor as yourself" (2:8). James is not advocating some kind of emotional affection for oneself. Self-love is clearly a sin (2 Timothy 3:2). Rather, the command is to pursue meeting the physical health and spiritual well-being of one's neighbors (all who are within the sphere of our influence; Luke 10:30-37) with the same intensity and concern as one does naturally for oneself (Philippians 2:3-4).[23]

As you concentrate on fulfilling the royal law and loving your neighbor as yourself, you will want to consider the "neighbors" whom you could demonstrate impartiality to—singles, widows, and individuals experiencing financial insecurity (low incomes, poverty level, and the homeless).

Single is defined as "pertaining to the unmarried state."[24] The December 1, 2004, edition of *USA Today* reports:

> *Census Bureau figures for 2003 show one-third of men and nearly one-quarter of women between the ages of 30 and 34 have never been married, nearly four times the rates in 1970.*[25]

When you plan social gatherings, do you embrace impartiality and include singles? More than likely their life experiences are rich, and they will enhance them.

A widow is "a woman who has lost her husband by death and has not remarried."[26] First Timothy 5:3-16 provides a clear definition of a Christian widow and specific instructions on how the church is to respond to her if she has no means of providing for her daily needs. National bereavement statistics reported by the American Association of Retired People (AARP) tell us that:

- In 1999, almost half (45 percent) of women over sixty-five were widows. Nearly 700,000 women lose their husbands each year and will be widows for an average of fourteen years (U.S. Bureau of the Census).
- The average monthly benefit for non-disabled widow(er)s was $812 in February 2000 (Social Security Administration).

- In 1999, there were more than four times as many widows (8.4 million) as widowers (1.9 million).[27]

As with the single woman, the widow possesses a wealth of life experiences that will enhance your social gathering. In the beginning of the grieving process, she may not be the life of the party, but your invitation, extended with a heart of impartiality, may allow her recovery process to accelerate. Remember, as a believer, you are instructed to be sensitive and compassionate to the pain and sorrows of others (Romans 12:15; Colossians 3:12). And there is a 50/50 chance that one day you will be in the same situation (Galatians 6:7).[28]

Food security is a twenty-first-century term that describes whether or not an individual has access, at all times, to enough food for an active, healthy life. We are more familiar with terms like *low income, poverty level, or the homeless*, which all describe food insecurity. This term should touch your heart when you consider that our Lord Jesus, during His earthly ministry, was in essence a homeless person (Matthew 8:20; 2 Corinthians 8:9).

According to the USDA Hunger Report:

- Eighty-nine percent of American household were food secure throughout 2002.
- The remaining households were food insecure for at least some time during that year.
- The prevalence of food insecurity rose from 10.7 percent in 2001 to 11.1 percent in 2002, while the prevalence of food insecurity rose from 3.3 percent to 3.5 percent.[29]

While our pantries may not always be filled with all the delicacies that our palates might desire, most of us have an adequate food supply. We can embrace impartiality by designating a portion of our grocery budget each month to those who encounter food insecurity.

Your opportunities to display impartiality are limitless. If you are going to make your faith practical (James 1:17), you will consider:

- nurturing the abandoned (Exodus 2:6-10).
- providing material needs (2 Samuel 17:27-29).
- weeping, mourning, and praying with others, and, when appropriate, fasting for them (Nehemiah 1:1-11).
- sharing your faith with the spiritually bankrupt (Matthew 11:28-30).
- encouraging the weak and oppressed (Isaiah 40:11; 42:3; Matthew 12:18-21).
- assisting with the needs of the infirmed (Luke 7:13; John 11:33, 35).
- modeling biblical compassion (Mark 8:1-2).

As you reflect on singles, widows, and individuals experiencing food insecurity, you will want to consider that one day your life's circumstances may plunge you into one of these categories. If that were to happen, would you be like my friend Melinda, whose consistent extension of graciousness and impartiality provided her with a support group drawn from a wide assortment of ages, professional standings, and social circles? If your response is not affirmative, may I challenge you to begin this day, through the strength of the Lord, to make a concerted effort to fulfill the greatest commandment (Matthew 22:34-39; Mark 12:28-34)?

Developing a Gentle and Quiet Spirit

Scriptures to Study

> Matthew 7:12; 22:34-39; Mark 12:28-34; James 2:1-17

For Meditation

> Proverbs 31:20

For Further Study

- Study Matthew 7:12, Matthew 22:34-39, and Mark 12:28-34. How do these verses challenge you to measure your love for others by what you wish for yourself?

- Investigate the impartiality modeled by the Lord Jesus (Isaiah 40:11; 42:3; Matthew 4:2; 9:36; 11:28-30; 12:18-21; 14:13-21; Mark 1:41; 6:31-44; 8:1-2; Luke 7:13; 9:11-17; 19:41; John 3:16; Hebrews 5:2, 7). List practical ways that you can practice impartiality in your community. Prayerfully ask our heavenly Father to help you integrate one of them.

- The wise woman of Proverbs 31 willingly "extends her hands to the poor" and "reaches out her hands to the needy" (Proverbs 31:20 NKJV). List the tasks she performed. Describe her attitude as she practiced impartiality. List any changes you would need to make to your life to follow her example.

A Principle to Ponder

> Precious in His sight is the woman who seeks to fulfill "the royal law according to the Scripture" (James 2:8) and loves her neighbor as herself (Matthew 22:37–40, 2:1-17).

12

Precious in His Sight is...

The Woman Who Chooses to be a Spiritual Mother

For all eternity, may happiness and peace be as abundant in your
heart as your goodness and sweetness so rightfully deserves...
The LORD will give strength unto His people;
The LORD will bless His people with peace.
Psalm 29:11

*S*o reads the inscription written by my father to my mother in her Bible eight years prior to my adoption into the Ennis family. My mother's prayer was much like Hannah's recorded in 1 Samuel 1:10-19. She greatly desired a child; however, a hysterectomy at an early age rendered the desire biologically impossible. The Lord, nonetheless, said yes to her heart's desire and allowed the assimilation of a daughter into their childless household through adoption.

Certainly He knew what type of parents I would need. An abandoned child with very poor health, I would not have survived in a household where I was not tenderly monitored. My parents had already done their "fun things" as a couple and were happy to stay at home and nurture the child for whom they had earnestly prayed.

Mother impacted my life in multiple ways. Those making the greatest contribution include:

- Teaching me by example to be a "keeper at home." Mother loved her home and made it a prepared place for those who belonged there. She spent time transferring her skills and abilities to me rather than simply doing the tasks and allowing me to enjoy them.

- Practicing patience while I learned the skills. She performed the tasks skillfully. It would have been easy for her, especially at her age, to become impatient and critical with a novice.

- Being at home when I arrived. We shared many special times because she anticipated my homecoming and willingly gave me her undivided attention.

- Allowing my friends to come to our home.

- Transferring godly values and standards that would guide me during the years when I would not have parental influence. (My mother went to be with the Lord when I was twenty-three, and my father when I was eighteen).

- Willingly sacrificing for me in material resources, time, and energy.

- Displaying the attributes of love rather than just talking about them.

As you read this description of my mother, numerous thoughts may be filtering through your mind. *I have (or had) a mother like that. Or, My mother was not anything like what you described. Or, I am single (or have not been able to conceive), so what you wrote does not apply to me.* You are blessed if your mother was a mirror image of mine. But you have no reason for self-pity if our gracious heavenly Father said no to a godly mother, husband, or children. Regardless of your heritage or marital status, if you are a Christian, Titus 2:3-5 clearly instructs you to be a spiritual mother.

Let's examine some of the basic virtues you are to exemplify, using the letters that form the word *mother* as our foundation:

M   modeling the character qualities that you want your spiritual
       daughters to embrace (1 Corinthians 4:16; 11:1).

O   obedient to those having authority over you (Hebrews 13:17).

T   teachable (Psalms 27:11, 86:11) and capable of teaching
       (2 Timothy 2:24; Titus 2:4).

H   humble (Proverbs 16:19; Isaiah 57:15).

E   exhorting and encouraging (1 Thessalonians 5:14;
       Hebrews 3:13; 10:19-25).

R   reputation for good works (Proverbs 31:29; 1 Timothy 5:3-10).

Despite the fact that Titus 2:3-5 is an instruction, not a suggestion, few Christian women are willing to assume the role of spiritual mother. Excuses range from "I don't know that much" to "No one cares what I have to say," or "I don't have the time." However, when a spiritual mother hides behind these excuses, she is sinning by failing to obey a clear instruction from her heavenly Father. An excuse is not a substitute for obedience (1 Samuel 15:22). The woman who is precious in God's sight joyfully practices this biblical instruction.

Spiritual mothering must move beyond simply having tea together or pursuing a one-on-one Bible study. If it is defined only as teaching or studying a book together, the importance of relationship so critical to spiritual parenting is missed. Just as providing physical nourishment is characteristic of biological parenting, so imparting spiritual nourishment is vital to being a spiritual mother.

Verna Birkey, my spiritual mother, writes in *Women Connecting with Women*, "Nourishment, then, is something that feeds my soul hunger so that life will be full, healthy and growing, instead of fainting and ebbing away."[30] The spiritual mother offers nourishment through encouragement, admonition, and reproof.

Encourage is derived from the Greek word *protrepo*, meaning "to urge forward or to persuade."[31] The spiritual mother acknowledges that though the spiritual daughter is benefiting from her experience, one day she may surpass her. The spiritual mother's attitude is like that of John in relation to the Lord Jesus: "He must increase, but I must decrease" (John 3:30). She becomes her spiritual daughter's strongest cheerleader.

Admonition is the Greek word *nouthesia,* meaning "training by word, whether of encouragement, or, if necessary, by reproof or remonstrance."[32] Colossians 3:16 instructs believers "to let the message about the Messiah dwell richly among you, teaching and admonishing one another in all wisdom, and singing psalms, hymns, and spiritual songs, with gratitude in your hearts towards God" (Col. 3:16–17). The spiritual mother will use the Word of God as a source for any admonition.

Elegmos, the Greek word for "reproof," refers to conviction or rebuke. Second Timothy 3:16-17 provides the biblical pattern for reproof. "All Scripture is breathed out by God and profitable for teaching, for reproof, for correction, and for training in righteousness, that the man of God may be competent, equipped for every good work."

Today I chair the Home Economics Department at a Christian college that is based on the Titus 2:3-5 precept. It is the second college program based on Titus 2:3-5 I have established. Much of what I impart to my students is generated from the foundation I received through my adopted and spiritual mothers' training and example.

Developing a Gentle and Quiet Spirit

Scriptures to Study

1 Kings 22:51-52; Psalm 113:9; Isaiah 66:13; Ezekiel 16:44-45; 1 Timothy 2:9-12, 15, 5:14; 1 Peter 3:3-6

For Meditation

Titus 2:3-5

For Further Study

- Investigate the mothers of the Bible. Consider Hagar (Genesis 21:9-21), Rebekah (Genesis 24:1-28; Romans 9:6-16), Leah (Genesis 29:16-35), Rachel (Genesis 35:16-2; Jeremiah 31:15), and Jochebed (Exodus 2:1-10; 6:20) as a starting point for your study.

- Create your own spiritual MOTHER acrostic following the model provided in this chapter. Be sure to include the basic virtues you are to exemplify as you assume the role of a spiritual mother. Acknowledge that you cannot assimilate the virtues in your own strength. Consistently pray that our heavenly Father will strengthen you to do so (Philippians 4:13).

- Elizabeth exemplified strength of character and served as a spiritual mother to Mary. As you study Luke 1:5-45, identify specific examples of her nurturing of Mary. How can you follow her model?

A Principle to Ponder

Precious in His sight is the woman who joyfully embraces the Titus 2:3-5 precept.

13

Precious in His Sight is...

The Woman Who Honors Her Earthly Father

A blonde-headed, blue-eyed daughter, I looked like the perfect blend of my mother and father. As others commented on the likeness, my parents smiled knowing that their heavenly Father had chosen the custom matching of their adopted daughter as He had made "a home for the lonely" (Psalm 68:6 NASB) or, according to the King James Version, had set another solitary in a family.

Oliver and Mary Ennis were older than most prospective parents when they commenced the adoption process, but they were willing to commit to nurturing a child. Eventually they welcomed to their home an abandoned child with pneumonia—me.

Most children spend at least eighteen years with one or both of their parents. My folks knew it was unlikely that they would enjoy the normal number because of their age and declining health, so they maximized each year to its fullest.

Though both of my parents made a significant imprint on my character, when Father's Day approaches I am reminded of the importance of honoring my earthly father. Honor means not simply outward compliance but inward respect that motivates sincere obedience.

My father's nurturing of me (Ephesians 6:1) promoted my cultivating an attitude of respect toward him. May I share several examples with you?

Love was characteristic of my father's relationship with me. He chose to train me by spending time with me. A busy realtor by profession, he would leave his office once a week and take me to the San Diego Zoo to participate in one of my favorite pastimes: feeding (and chasing) the peacocks. From playing games to picnics, worship to dining out as a family, my childhood was filled with rich experiences. . . and Dad was usually there. He drove for field trips, helped with Girl Scout activities, and transported me to school each day. The times in the car allowed us to talk about many things, allowing him to share life principles without preaching sermons.

Discipline was practiced in our home. Through Dad's training I learned early that I was the loser if I pushed my will. He cared enough to say no and was not swayed by my tears. He insisted that I look into his eyes when he talked with me, whatever the topic of discussion. There were times when I wanted to look anywhere else but into his eyes. The transfer to look into my heavenly Father's eyes was easy because of Dad's early training.

Celebrations were important in the Ennis household. . . and Dad was the catalyst of many of them. I recall well a January day when I was ten. I arrived at home and found the dining room table set with Mom's best linen and china. Lying across my bed was a fancy new dress and my favorite black patent leather shoes. My mother helped me dress for dinner. When Dad arrived, dressed in his best suit, a special dinner was served.

He then began the explanation for the celebration. January 31 was the day they brought me home from the hospital, six months after my birth. I was not their biological child, but I was very special because they had chosen me.

His explanation made my subsequent transition to salvation smooth. Salvation was like being adopted into God's family. How could I not desire heavenly adoption when my earthly adoption was so wonderful?

Dad took me on my first date and taught me how a lady should be treated. He always gave me a choice about telling my male escort what time I needed to be home, but before I left, the information was clearly communicated. He taught me to respect my mother, first by example, then by insistence.

Both parents were conservative in clothing choices. However, there were garments I could get Mom to approve that Dad would not allow—explaining why the choice was not a good one from a man's perspective. He affirmed the godly character and skills that my mother possessed and encouraged me to assimilate them. Mom was an excellent cook, and my dad ate many questionable meals as I learned to emulate her skills.

Illness took him out of the work force prematurely. Doctors predicted he would be fortunate to live until I graduated from high school. Yet he continued to do all that he could to prepare me for the future. He insisted on college. He taught me how to develop a budget, balance a checkbook, and complete income tax forms because he knew that much of the financial responsibility of our home would become my responsibility when he was ushered into eternity. Through the advanced stages of emphysema, he modeled patience and trust in his heavenly Father.

The Lord granted his wish to live until I graduated from high school—Dad went home to be with Him my second day of college.

Mother lived five years beyond Dad and saw the answer to her prayer that I would have professional employment. She joined my Father in heaven my second day of teaching.

Chronologically, I spent fewer years with my parents than most children do. But because of their careful instruction, I was able to transition to placing my trust in my gracious heavenly Father (1 Peter 5:7).

You may not have the heritage of a godly father that I have. But if you are a believer, you have a heavenly Father who loves you even more than my earthly father loved me. Let's review some of His qualities using an acrostic from the word FATHER and personalize it by saying, "My heavenly Father is...

F   faithful (Deuteronomy 7:9; 1 Corinthians 1:9, 10:13; 1 Peter 4:19)

A   available (Psalms 9:12b; 34:15b; Isaiah 58:9; 65:24; Zechariah 13:9)

T   my Teacher (Psalms 25:4; 27:11; 86:11; 90:12; 94:12;
    Isaiah 2:3; 28:9-10, 17, 26.)

H   holy (Leviticus 19:1-3; 20:7; 21:8; Psalms 22:3; 99:9; 145:17;
    Isaiah 5:16; 6:3; John 17:11)

E   eternal (Deuteronomy 33:27; Psalm 90:2; Revelation 4:8-10)

R   my Refuge (Deuteronomy 33:27; 2 Samuel 22:3; Psalms 9:9; 46:1;
    57:1; 59:16; 71:7; 94:22)

What type of relationship do you have with your earthly father? Though he may not model perfection, do you choose to honor him by affirming his positive character qualities (Philippians 4:8-9)? Do you view his weaknesses through the lens that each one has a potential strength? Do you pray that he will allow the Lord to transform them to strengths (Mark 10:27)?

Crafting your own acrostic from the word FATHER is a helpful way to do that. Here are some suggestions based on the relationship I shared with my father to stimulate your thought processes:

Faithful   Thank you, Dad, for your example of faithfulness.

Adopted   Thank you for integrating me into your family when no one else wanted me.

Teach   Thank you for teaching me by principle and example.

Heritage   Thank you for giving me a rich heritage of training and memories to cushion the years when I would be without family.

Endurance   Thank you for teaching me to endure, without complaining, even when the circumstances appear insurmountable. I am a finisher because you were.

Respect   Thank you for insisting that I demonstrate respect and for teaching me that submitting to authority is a way to model respect.

May I challenge you, when the season to honor fathers arrives, to extend gratitude to both your earthly father and your heavenly Father? Doing so will revolutionize your life!

∞

Developing a Gentle and Quiet Spirit

Scriptures to Study
> Exodus 20:12; Deuteronomy 5:16; Matthew 15:4; 19:19;
> Mark 7:10; 10:19; Luke 18:20; Ephesians 6:2

For Meditation
> Proverbs 1:8-9

For Further Study
- Scripture challenges believers to honor a variety of categories of individuals, including God (Psalm 29:2; 71:8), parents (Exodus 20:12; Deuteronomy 5:16; Ephesians 6:2), the aged (Leviticus 19:32), and those in leadership (1 Peter 2:17). Use the references provided as a springboard to investigate how these people are to be honored. What steps will you take to integrate these individuals in your life?
- Create your own heavenly FATHER acrostic following the model provided in this chapter. Remember to personalize it by saying, "My heavenly Father is..."
- Jephthah's daughter is an example of a young woman who displayed gracious support of her devastated father and courageously submitted to God's will (Judges 10-11). What lessons can you learn from her life?

A Principle to Ponder
> Precious in His sight is the woman who extends gratitude
> to both her heavenly Father and her earthly father
> (1 Thessalonians 5:18).

14

Precious in His Sight is...
The Woman Who Offers Trust and Confidence
in Her Friendships

T dial the phone, the answering machine responds, I hear my beloved friend's voice. I knew she would not be at home. You see, I am calling to inquire about the physical condition that prompted her admission to the hospital several days prior to the new year. Having experienced a reaction to her most recent chemotherapy treatment, she is in an unconscious state. The fact that her husband is not answering the phone tells me that he is probably still at her bedside.

Memories flood my mind as I recall her kindness as a friend—always urging me to reach my full professional potential, investing her time and resources to assist in my success, offering advice and counsel, editing my writing endeavors, telling me the truth when content needed to be revised, and simply having fun together are a few of the things that comprise our friendship collage. Once again I ponder—Was I careful to express my gratitude and thanks for her faithfulness that spanned some thirty years? *Dear Lord, I pray, if it would please You, provide me with the opportunity to communicate to Barbara how much I treasure her friendship.*

The days pass, and then one evening her husband answers the phone with the blessed report. "Barbara is with us again!" As I offer my heartfelt thanks to my heavenly Father, I am motivated to make certain that I communicate to her regularly the depth and breadth of our friendship.

One of the classic descriptions of friendship recorded in Scripture is that of Jonathan and David (1 Samuel 18:1-4, 19, 20; 23:16; 2 Samuel 1:17). Let's consider some of the qualities of their relationship that provide a role model for us:

- Friendship requires initiation (18:1). In our twenty-first-century society, too many friendships are based on surface attributes and selfish ambitions. Jonathan's initiation of his friendship with David reflects a willingness to cross social barriers and personal agendas to develop a genuine relationship.
- Friendship involves sacrifice (18:4; 23:16-17). Unselfishness is necessary to practice true friendship. Each individual must be willing to give up something treasured; in Jonathan's case, he willingly surrendered his rightful position as king.
- Friendship promotes the best interests of the other. Jeopardizing his own safety and his relationship with his father, Jonathan sought to alert David to potential danger (19:1-2), defend him, and cultivate a spirit of reconciliation between Saul and David (19:3-7).
- Friendship is willing to take the brunt of another person's circumstances (20:24-33). Every person needs someone to "go to the wall" for her. Against insurmountable odds, Jonathan went to the wall for David. Second Samuel 1:26 clearly shows that David's love for Jonathan was reciprocated. Writing about their relationship, John MacArthur states, "A deep concern and affection was the basis of the covenantal relationship between Jonathan and David. This is the affection commanded by God when He said, 'Love your neighbor as yourself.'"[33]

Your friends should sense a spirit of trust and confidence in the shared relationship. When I consider the characteristics of trust and confidence that I should manifest as a friend, I am reminded that Elizabeth's life[34] serves as the type of model I desire to follow (Luke 1:39-56). Let's take a look at what her life teaches us about trustworthiness and confidence as we see how she responded to her friend Mary, who was experiencing personal challenges.

- Mary had confidence that she would be welcome in Elizabeth's home. She had no way of alerting Elizabeth of her intention to come for an extended visit (Luke 1:39-40).

- Mary chose to share freely her situation with Elizabeth, a relative as well as an older woman. This suggests that Mary trusted Elizabeth to believe the best rather than the worst about her (Luke 1:40).

- Elizabeth waited for Mary to share the reason for her visit rather than immediately interrogating her (Luke 1:40b-41) or preempting the situation by sharing her good news.

- Elizabeth was a clean vessel that the Holy Spirit could use to affirm the Lord's work in Mary's life (Luke 1:41).

- Elizabeth offered extended hospitality to Mary (Luke 1:56). Since Mary arrived when Elizabeth was six months pregnant, she evidently stayed until John the Baptist was born—not the most convenient time for a long-term guest.

Friendship is one of the most precious of God's gifts to us. May I encourage you to evaluate your friendship garden and discern how you are nurturing it? The following piece of poetry provides a wonderful stimulus to begin the evaluation.

My Greatest Prize
by Janet Ritchie

It seems as each year ends,
I look back and think of my friends,
What I did right, what I did wrong,
Who came into my life and who is gone.

But every year there are those who remain,
Looking only for friendship; nothing else to gain.
They have stayed by me through good and bad,
Smiled when I am happy, held me when I've been sad.

After so many years you begin to realize
That a friend is life's greatest prize,
Not the pot of gold at the end of a rainbow
That we seem to seek wherever we go.

So as I grow older and begin another New Year's Day,
I will thank God for those friends He sent my way.
And my New Year's resolution will always be
To thank Him again for every breath of life He's given me.

Then I will pray He will show me the way,
Give me wisdom and guide me through each day.
And most of all, at the end of each year,
Keep by me those friends I will always hold so dear.
And as I make new friends, I'll treasure the old,
For the first are silver, the latter gold.[35]

Developing a Gentle and Quiet Spirit

Scriptures to Study

1 Samuel 18:1-4; 19:1-7; 2 Samuel 1:26; 20:24-33; Luke 1:39-56

For Meditation

Proverbs 17:17

For Further Study

- Numerous Scriptures provide descriptions of the behaviors that a friend should practice. Use Ephesians 5:21, Colossians 3:13, and 1 Thessalonians 5:11, 14 as a foundation for the response to the question "As a woman who desires to be precious in God's sight, what qualities should I exhibit as a friend?"

- Proverbs 17:17 and 18:24 teach us that a friend wisely chosen can be more valuable than a relative. What qualities do you possess that would allow these verses to describe you? What changes will you ask your heavenly Father to make in your life so that these verses are more descriptive of you?

- Elizabeth modeled Proverbs 17:17 and 18:24 by choosing to be a friend who loved at all times. As you study Luke 1:39-56, list Elizabeth's actions and attitudes that demonstrate her application of the Proverbs verses.

A Principle to Ponder

Precious in His sight is the woman who nurtures her friendships— one of His most precious gifts to her (John 15:13).

15

Precious in His Sight is...

The Woman Who Offers Acknowledges Her Need For Womanly Companionship

And a youth said, Speak to us of Friendship. And he answered, saying: Your friend is your needs answered. He is your field which you sow with love and reap with thanksgiving. And he is your board and your fireside. For you come to him with your hunger, and you seek him for peace.

When your friend speaks his mind you fear not the "nay" in your own mind, nor do you withhold the "ay." And when he is silent your heart ceases not to listen to his heart;

For without words, in friendship, all thoughts, all desires, all expectations are born and shared, with joy that is unclaimed. When you part from your friend, you grieve not; for that which you love most in him may be clearer in his absence, as the mountain to the climber is clearer from the plain.

And let there be no purpose in friendship save the deepening of the spirit. For love that seeks aught but the disclosure of its own mystery is not love but a net cast forth: and only the unprofitable is caught.

And let your best be for your friend. If he must know the ebb of your tide, let him know its flood also. For what is your friend that you should seek him with hours to kill? Seek him always with hours to live. For it is his to fill your need, but not your emptiness. And in the sweetness of friendship let there be laughter, and sharing of pleasures.

For in the dew of little things the heart finds its morning and is refreshed.[36]

—*Kahlil Gibran*

As you read the title of this chapter and the introductory poem, were you able to identify one or more individuals whom you consider true friends? Or do you fall into the dilemma described by Beverly LaHaye?

Everyone is busy these days, few have the time to develop friendships. We're on a fast-moving treadmill, and as we go to work, organize, and run our household, chauffeur our children, and stay busy at church, we cut corners to save time. Along the way, we begin to neglect the women we have known as friends.[37]

If we are honest, most of us long for the kind of "kindred spirit" friend so eloquently described by Anne Shirley in the classic story of an orphan girl, *Anne of Green Gables*.[38] Her longing is replicated in the hearts of women everywhere because, as Ecclesiastes 4:9-12 teaches, we all have a built-in need for companionship.

Numerous research studies reinforce what Anne Shirley and Solomon, the author of Ecclesiastes 4:9-10, taught centuries ago. "Two are better than one, because they have a good reward for their toil. For if they fall, one will lift up his fellow. But woe to him who is alone when he falls and has not another to lift him up!"

A landmark UCLA study suggests that friends help us live better and longer. This UCLA study cited the famed Nurses' Health Study from Harvard Medical School, which found that the more friends women had, the less likely they were to develop physical impairments as they aged, and the more likely they were to lead joyful lives. In fact, the results were so significant, the researchers concluded that not having close friends or confidants was as detrimental to one's health as smoking or carrying extra weight.

When researchers evaluated how well women functioned after the deaths of their spouses, they found that even in the midst of the biggest of life's stressors, women who had a close friend and confidant were more likely to survive the experience without any new physical impairment or permanent loss of vitality. Those without friends were not always so fortunate.[39]

While these research findings help you understand of your need for friends, a brief journey through Scripture reveals the significant impact that true friends can make on your life. Friends, according to Scripture:

- refresh one another, and in turn provide personal refreshment (Proverbs 11:25)
- greatly influence us (Proverbs 13:20)
- love you enough to tell you the things you don't want to hear in a way that you can accept them (Proverbs 16:21)
- refuse to entertain the words of a slanderer (Proverbs 16:28)
- can be more loyal than family members (Proverbs 18:24)
- help you to see where you fall short of doing God's will (Proverbs 27:6)
- offer wise counsel because their overriding motive is to seek your long-term good (Proverbs 27:9)
- are available in time of need (Proverbs 27:10)
- choose to be reconciled to one another before attempting to worship their heavenly Father (Matthew 5:24)
- forgive one another (Matthew 6:14)
- reveal their relationship with God by their interaction with you. John 13:35 says, "By this all people will know that you are my disciples, if you have love for one another."
- can mold your life toward wisdom or foolishness (1 Corinthians 15:33).
- encourage, challenge, and hold you accountable (Galatians 6:2)
- meet your needs in specific ways (Galatians 6:10)
- speak the truth in love (Ephesians 4:15)
- help you see the true, honorable, right, pure, lovely, excellent, and praiseworthy qualities of life (Philippians 4:8-9)
- are visible examples of God's sacrificial love toward mankind (John 13:34-35; 1 John 4:7).

Based on the findings of our scriptural journey, it is safe to conclude that the key to developing long-term friendships is to balance love's tough and tender sides. The "tough" side provides protection and confrontation, while the "tender" side offers sympathy, affirmation, and encouragement.

The rose, the flower most frequently associated with love in our culture, provides a wonderful visual of the "tough and tender" aspects of friendship. The thorns of the rose, its toughness, protect and augment it without detracting from its beauty. Its tender side is found in its velvety petals that minister in a quiet, unassuming way, and its fragrance gently reminds us of its presence. What characterizes the beauty of the rose is also true in our friendships. The tough side does what is best for one's friend regardless of the immediate personal sacrifice. If someone is truly your friend, she will endeavor to consistently nurture the relationship, confront when necessary, challenge you to reach your full potential, and defend you. The tender side offers you unconditional love, attempts to understand your feelings even though she may disagree with them, listens without condemnation, and willingly says, "I was wrong; will your forgive me?"

As we conclude our study of the importance of women developing relationships with one another, may I pose a question for you to ponder? If female companionship counters so many of the negative aspects of life in the twenty-first century, keeps you healthy, and may even add years to your life, why is it so difficult to carve out the time for it? As you contemplate your response, consider our Lord Jesus, who set the standard for unchanging, steadfast love and commitment in friendship (Hebrews 13:6). If you seek to emulate His example, you will undoubtedly find your capacity to "love your neighbor as yourself" increasing (Leviticus 19:18; Deuteronomy 6:5; Matthew 22:37-40). Are you willing, through His strength, to build friendships that reflect that you are a friend with God, the almighty Creator of all?

Developing a Gentle and Quiet Spirit

Scriptures to Study

Proverbs 18:24; 27:6, 9-10; John 13:34-35; 15:12-17; 1 John 4:7

For Meditation

Ecclesiastes 4:9-12

For Further Study

- As you read the title of this chapter and the introductory poem, were you able to identify one or more individuals whom you consider to be true friends? Do you nurture or neglect these ladies? Use specific examples as you respond to this question.

- Cultivating a deep friendship with God is the foundation of developing quality relationships with others. Search the Scriptures to discern how to become a friend of God. These will get you started: Exodus 33:11; 2 Chronicles 20:7; Job 29:4; John 15:14-15. A chart format like the one below might prove helpful to you.

SCRIPTURE REFERENCE	CHARACTERISTICS OF THE RELATIONSHIP	WAYS I CAN MODEL THE RELATIONSHIP
Exodus 33:11		
2 Chronicles 20:7		
Job 29:4		
John 15:14-15		

- Ruth and Naomi's relationship provides a wonderful example of an intergenerational (women of different generations) friendship (Ruth 1-4). What qualities can you glean from their relationship that provide a foundation for the relationships that you cultivate?

A Principle to Ponder

Precious in His sight is the woman who acknowledges that she needs to cultivate female friendships (Ecclesiastes 4:9-12).

16

Precious in His Sight is...

The Woman Who Cultivates Her Friendship Garden

When you consider cultivating your friendship garden, what level of time, energy, and resources do you expect to invest? *Cultivation* means to "promote or improve the growth of a plant or crop by labor and attention."[40] For example, if I am going to produce quality roses, there are some basic procedures to follow. I must begin with healthy bushes, plant them in a sunny, well-drained location, provide them with proper nutrition, mulch them (supply a protective covering to prevent excessive water evaporation or erosion) during the summer months, furnish disease prevention and control, prune them at the proper time, and shelter them in the winter.[41] Even with such tender care, there may be times that I may experience a less than profuse rose garden.

Similarly, if I want to contribute to a healthy friendship garden, I need to invest time, energy, and resources. Second Corinthians 9:6 provides a simple agrarian principle that the harvest one receives is directly proportional to the amount and quality of seed sown, while Galatians 6:7-10 reminds us that we will reap what we sow. Writing on Galatians 6:10, John MacArthur states that "our love for fellow Christians is the primary test of our love for God."[42]

- Take the time to truly know your friends. This means learning how to share yourself intimately and appropriately, sharing at the same level of disclosure your friend is sharing, moving into intimate sharing slowly, and exhibiting a willingness to share strengths and weaknesses, failures and fears, as well as victories and successes.

- Wholeheartedly listen to the person when she is speaking—even if you think she is going to tell you something you don't want to hear. Often when a friend begins to communicate something we are not excited about knowing, our first reaction is to build our defense rather than completely tracking with her.

- Be trustworthy. The first quality suggested of the wise woman of Proverbs 31 (Proverbs 31:12) is that she "does him good." While this principle is placed in the context of the marriage relationship, it is the same for all relationships. You are to do all that is in your power to improve the other person's life, seek to help her develop her potential to the fullest, and not compete, but assist her in doing the work and will of God. Refusing to "do harm" includes defending your friend, never betraying or slandering her, striving to keep promises, never telling others what she has shared with you in confidence, and not breaking her spirit by unnecessary criticism. You will also not desert her by withdrawing your acceptance of her, make your acceptance conditional upon her complying or cooperating with you or conforming to your standards, and not withholding your interest or care when you do not have an immediate need for her in your life. If a woman cannot be a trustworthy friend, it is unlikely she will be a trustworthy spouse since "practice makes perfect."

- Purpose to practice consistency in your relationships—even when you do not feel like it. If you are going to follow the

Do you have hot/cold friends where you never know where you stand with that person?

biblical model for friendships, you will choose to love at all times (Proverbs 17:17). This means that your warmth toward your friends is to be unswerving, that you regularly communicate that you like them—even when you don't approve of their choices.

- Work hard to ensure that you are doing your part to maintain the relationship. When you neglect to invest time and effort in a relationship, you are essentially saying, "I don't care very much." Maintaining the relationship suggests that you are a forgiving person (Colossians 3:13-14), willing to bear with the weaknesses and idiosyncrasies of others (1 Corinthians 13:7), and quick to clear up misunderstandings as soon as they arise (Mark 10:25-26; Galatians 6:1). It also means dealing with your pride and asking forgiveness when you have offended your friend (Matthew 5:23-24; 6:14-15) and surrendering your desire to punish her when she has hurt or upset you (2 Timothy 2:23-26). True friendship freely grants forgiveness (Ephesians 4:31-32) and forgets transgressions (Psalm 103:12; Jeremiah 31:34).

You will probably not experience the same level of intimacy in each relationship you cultivate. Looking at a description of the phases of friendship may help you apply the principles that we have established by using the visual of the phases of a rose.

Phase One—The Green Bud

As with the rose when it is wrapped in its green shroud, the knowledge of your friend is vague at the Green Bud phase. You know who the person is and perhaps some basic information about her. Our wise heavenly Father brings a variety of temperaments together to sharpen one another in friendships (Proverbs 27:17). Sometimes the friends will be very similar; other times they will be different. Regardless of the temperaments of the ladies, the Green Bud phase begins with respect for each other. Though one of you will probably need to initiate the relationship, the other can demonstrate that she is available.

Phase Two—The Emerging Bud

It is always exciting to observe the green shroud slowly unfold to reveal the potential beauty of the rose petals. Experience teaches that if the process is preempted by human assistance, the petals emerge earlier, but are often damaged. The same is true in budding friendships. Time and patience are necessary for the Green Bud phase to transition to the Emerging Bud phase.

Characteristic of the Emerging Bud phase is knowing more about your friend, her interests, what she does and does not enjoy doing, perhaps some future goals, and a bit about her past. Essentially you know not only who she is, but what she is like. Though you may do things together— perhaps work together, talk about interests together, and occasionally ask each other for help—generally there is little commitment or much deep, intimate sharing.

Phase Three—The Unfurled Rose

Given the proper climate and conditions, the Emerging Bud phase gently opens up to reveal the depth of the relationship distinctive of the Unfurled Rose phase. The true character of the friendship is revealed in this phase since you know your friend in greater depth due to the time commitment and intimate sharing that has occurred. The Unfurled Rose phase necessitates a variety of shared interests. The values the friends embrace are similar. The friends assume mutual responsibility to keep the relationship on track and growing.

Nourishment is characteristic of the Unfurled Rose phase. Verna Birkey writes in *Women Connecting with Women*, "Nourishment, then, is something that feeds my soul hunger so that life will be full, healthy and growing, instead of fainting and ebbing away."[43] Within this phase the friends offer nourishment to each other through affirmation, spiritual and emotional encouragement, and, when necessary, admonition and reproof.

Phase Four—The Full-Blown Rose

The genuine charm of a rose is discovered when it is full blown; likewise, the authenticity of a friendship is revealed in the Full Blown phase. Every now and then rosebuds start out healthy but droop, or their petals shatter, before they reach their maximum potential. The same is true in friendships. All will not mature into the Full Blown phase. However, those that do enjoy the unique quality of commitment that is the foundation of the Full Blown phase. You will enjoy the continued benefits of the characteristics of the Green Bud, Emerging Bud, and Unfurled Rose phases. But commitment prompts you to endure with your friend when she is preoccupied, is experiencing difficulty, or has failed. It means hanging in there under all circumstances, and staying with it when the well of spontaneous affection seems nearly dry. When your friendship reaches the Full Blown phase, you are committed to your friend's highest good—regardless of personal cost.

Love and reciprocal contribution encourage the Full Blown phase to flourish (Ecclesiastes 4:9-12). Warmth, communication of mutual concern and respect, and a willingness to accept each other demonstrate the presence of love. Each contributing to the maintenance of the relationship furthers its growth. Extending kindness to each other, forgiving each other (Ephesians 4:32), bearing with weaknesses and idiosyncrasies (Galatians 6:1-2), and reassuring each other will ensure that there are no weeds in your friendship garden.

Developing a Gentle and Quiet Spirit

Scriptures to Study

>Proverbs 31:11; Matthew 5:23-24; 6:14-15; Mark 10:25-26; John 13:35; Romans 12:10-13; 1 Corinthians 13; 2 Corinthians 9:6; Galatians 6:1, 7; Ephesians 4:31-32; 2 Timothy 2:23-26; 1 John 4:20-21

For Meditation

>Romans 12:10-13

For Further Study

- Numerous Scriptures describe behaviors that promote biblical friendships, including Proverbs 31:11, Matthew 5:23-24, 6:14-15, Mark 10:25-26, Romans 12:10-13, 1 Corinthians 13, 2 Corinthians 9:6, Galatians 6:1, 7, Ephesians 4:31-32, and 2 Timothy 2:23-26. Starting with these Scriptures, develop a "Friendship Chart" that helps you define the characteristics of a biblical friendship. Conduct your own research to locate additional Scriptures.

Scripture	Friendship Quality	Ways I Can Incorporate This Quality In My Life

- Consider the phases of friendship described in this chapter. Do you have friends at each level of intimacy? Are there any changes you need to make that will help you apply the friendship principles suggested in this chapter to your relationships?
- Mary and Martha chose to extend friendship to Jesus. How do Luke 10:38-42 and John 11:17-27, 32-44, and 12:1-11 describe the attributes of their friendship? What will you do to follow their example?

A Principle to Ponder

>Precious in His sight is the woman who conscientiously cultivates her friendship garden (Ephesians 4:32; Galatians 6:1-2; 1 Thessalonians 5:14).

17

Precious in His Sight is...

The Woman Who Weeds Her Friendship Garden

*S*ince female companionship counters so many of the negative aspects of life, keeps you healthy, and may even add years to your life, it is important to not only cultivate a friendship garden, but to consistently weed it. A weed is a plant that grows somewhere you don't want it—a simple definition for a potentially large problem. According to the Bureau of Land Management's Weeds Web site,[44] weeds fall into six categories: native or non-native, invasive or non-invasive, and noxious or not noxious. "Legally, a noxious weed is any plant designated by a federal, state or county government as injurious to public health, agriculture, recreation, wildlife or property."[45] A noxious weed is commonly defined as a plant that grows out of place (a rose can be a weed in a wheat field) and is "competitive, persistent, and pernicious."[46] Some invasive plants can produce significant changes to vegetation, composition, structure, or ecosystem function.

The most important way to fight weeds is to promote the best environment for the growth of desirable plants. Improper watering or fertilization, soil compaction, insect damage, disease, poor drainage, and improper sunlight all increase the potential for weed development.[47]

What is true of the care and maintenance of gardens is equally true in the nurturing of friendships. Relational weeds in the friendship garden have the potential of stunting or completely stopping growth. The book of John teaches that:

- ~~Loving others is a visual illustration of our discipleship~~ (13:34-35).
- Christians exemplify that they are friends with Christ when they love one another (15:14).
- Christians are to love one another as Christ loved them (15:12).
- ~~Loving one another is a command, not a suggestion, for Christians~~ ~~(15:17).~~

A variety of weeds can hinder the flourishing of love in the friendship garden, including:

The Turned-Head Weed

The Turned-Head Weed grows in one direction while its head faces the opposite direction. It might be called the "if only" weed because it lives on memories of other friendships and past experiences. It damages existing relationships by its continual reference to other, "more prosperous" relationships or by possessing unrealistic expectations of current ones. This weed is best eradicated by thanking God for precious memories and by concentrating on nurturing the current relationships He provides (Ephesians 5:20; Philippians 3:13; 1 Thessalonians 5:18).

The I-Me Weed

A fancy name for selfishness, the I-Me Weed grows to enormous heights until nothing else in the garden can be seen. It is a real love-choker, often turning friendships into thickets of fighting and competition. This weed creates an environment directly opposite of the agape love commanded by God that challenges you to accept your friend exactly as she is, forgives and forgets unintentional slights, places no demands on the friendship, and allows the will rather than the emotions to control it.

The I-Me Weed quickly establishes itself as the center of the friendship garden and demands to be in control. It is most effectively eradicated by sowing the Our-We seed in the friendship garden (Proverbs 13:10; Galatians 5:15; 19-25; Philippians 2:3; James 3:16).

The Clam-Up Weed

The Clam-Up Weed is one of the most difficult to eradicate because when one friend "clams up," it is almost impossible to correct the situation. Should this weed invade, the silence that falls over the friendship garden is like the silence of a tomb. The residual effect of this weed is often a suppression of one's feelings, which may eventually erupt in an explosion. To eradicate, communicate frequently and temper the tone, choice, and number of your words. Should disagreements arise, refuse to remain angry and be willing to admit your contribution to the conflict (Proverbs 25:11; 26:20; 31: 26; Ephesians 4:15, 25-32).

The Wandering Affection Weed

The Wandering Affection Weed is small, ugly, and has sharp leaves and roots that cut the roots of love under the surface, out of sight, so a relationship does not know what is happening until it is too late. This weed seeks to cultivate a new relationship by destroying an existing one. The Wandering Affection Weed whispers slanderous comments about existing friends, suggests that another friend can best fulfill your friendship needs, and insinuates that it is permissible to abort a long-established friendship for a new one. While it is important to pursue new friendships, it is not appropriate for you to undermine deeply rooted friendships to do so. Eradication of the Wandering Affection Weed includes refusing to discredit an existing friendship, purposing to "love at all times," seeking to bear your friend's burdens, doing things that are pleasing to her, and concentrating on her positive qualities rather than her weaknesses (Psalm 101:5; Proverbs 6:19; 17:17; Galatians 6:2, 10; Philippians 4:8-9).

The I Am Always Right Weed

Standing stiff and erect in the friendship garden, the friend possessing characteristics of the I Am Always Right Weed offers a sharp, immediate response to anything she disagrees with. Many ugly words can spew forth from her lips if she is provoked. When she assumes this stance of conflict, engaging in discussion with her is futile since she is always right. Eradication of the I Am Always Right Weed requires prayer on your part so that the words of your mouth and the meditations of your heart are acceptable to the Lord (Psalm 19:14). Filling your mind with God's Word so that your responses are His responses, and being willing to graciously and gently speak the truth in love, ensure that you are not providing ammunition that keeps a conflict in momentum. (See Psalms 19:14; 39:1; 49:3; 119:11; Proverbs 4:23-24; 10:20; 12:18; 15:2; 18:21; 21:23; 23:7; 25:21; 31:26; Matthew 12:33-37; Luke 6:45; Ephesians 4:14; Colossians 3:16; James 1:27-28; 3:6-10.)

The I Call You When I Need You Weed

The I Call You When I Need You Weed lies dormant for long periods and then emerges full grown when it desires to assert itself. Generating from the consumer mind-set of the twenty-first century, the I Call You When I Need You Weed extracts from the friendship what she desires, then allows it to lie latent until another need arises. As with the I-Me Weed, selfishness is the primary source of the I Call You When I Need You Weed. Eradication of this weed includes choosing to love your friend as yourself, being more concerned about her needs than yours, and praying for a heart that desires to honor others. (See Leviticus 19:18; Mathew 5:43; Mark 12:33; Romans 2:6-8; 12:10; 13:7; Philippians 2:3-4; Hebrews 13:1; 2 Peter 1:7-11.)

Regardless of the surface appearance of the weeds, all generate from the same taproot: pride, the first of the six things that the Lord hates (Proverbs 6:1). Pride cultivates disharmony in the friendship garden, while humility, the opposite of pride, generates an atmosphere of peace and harmony. The most effective time to eradicate weeds in the friendship garden is when they are young, tender, and actively growing—and you can only do this in the Lord's strength. As James 4:6, the spiritual weed killer, is applied to the invading weeds, your friendship garden will produce spectacular bouquets.

The Lord pleads in John 17:20-21, "I do not ask for these only, but also for those who will believe in me through their word, that they may all be one, just as you, Father, are in me, and I in you, that they also may be in us, so that the world may believe you have sent me." May you be quick to eradicate weeds from your friendship garden so that the watching world will observe the love of God in your friendships.

Developing a Gentle and Quiet Spirit

Scriptures to Study

John 4, 17

For Meditation

Ephesians 4:25-32

For Further Study

- John 13:34-35, 13:34-35, and 15:12-14, 17 are all passages that challenge believers to exemplify Christian love in their relationships. Study each, as well as the references cited with each weed description, then write a personal definition of how you can integrate their teaching into your relationships.

- Analyze Psalms 19:14, 39:1, 49:3, 119:11; Proverbs 4:23-24, 10:20, 12:18, 15:2, 18:21, 21:23, 23:7, 25:21, 31:26; Matthew 12:33-37; Luke 6:45; Ephesians 4:14; Colossians 3:16; and James 1:27-28, 3:6-10. Develop a set of Gracious Speech Guidelines that will challenge you to gently speak the truth in love regardless of the situation.

- Study the life of the Samaritan woman described in John 4. What relationship changes do you think she needed to make in order to cultivate a lasting relationship with Jesus? What about your relationships? Are there some that require modification in order to experience a more satisfying relationship with your Lord? Prayerfully place those modifications before your heavenly Father, and ask Him to give you the strength to make them. Be careful to express gratitude to Him as you experience the modifications.

A Principle to Ponder

Precious in His sight is the woman who consistently weeds her friendship garden (James 4:6).

18

Precious in His Sight is...

The Woman Who Evaluates the Quality of Friendship She Extends to Others

Only God knows what you are truly like. The remainder of those with whom you interact must be satisfied with what they see and hear from you (1 Samuel 16:7). The woman who seeks to cultivate friendships that please her heavenly Father chooses to carefully evaluate the characteristics of her friendships against the unchanging wisdom found in His Word.

This chapter was crafted to help you aerate the soil of your friendship garden by searching the Scriptures for "friendship wisdom" and then evaluating your garden's quality against God's ageless standards. As you study this chapter, follow these instructions to aerate the soil of your friendship garden:

- Read each category below along with each Scripture listed under it.
- Copy and answer the questions under each category. Provide specific examples to support your yes or no response.
- Read each additional Scripture and rewrite it into a question that provides a basis for you to evaluate your performance as a friend.
- Seek your own Scriptures to augment those provided for you.

My Relationship To My Friends

What kind of friend am I admonished to be?

- Proverbs 17:17—Do I love my friends at all times?
- Proverbs 18:24b—Am I available to my friends when they are experiencing difficult times?

  Suggested Scriptures for your questions: Proverbs 27:6;
  1 Corinthians 13:7; Galatians 5:14

What can ruin a friendship?

- Proverbs 16:28; 26:20—Do I gossip about or slander my friends?
- Proverbs 17:9—Do I intentionally share information with others who are neither part of the situation nor part of the solution?

  Suggested Scriptures for your questions: Proverbs 20:19;
  Psalm 15:2; Matthew 7:1-5

What kind of friend do I need?

- Proverbs 18:24—Do I have a friend who is more loyal than a family member? Do I display that kind of loyalty in my friendships?
- Galatians 5:22—Do I have friends who exhibit the fruit of the Spirit? Do I exhibit the fruit of the Spirit in my dealings with my friends?

  Suggested Scriptures for your questions: Ephesians 4:1-6, 29

Who wants to be that friend?

- John 15:14-15—Do I have a personal relationship with Jesus Christ?
- Matthew 10:37—Am I willing to invest the same energy in cultivating a strong friendship with Jesus Christ as I am investing in earthly friendships?

  Suggested Scriptures for your questions: Proverbs 17:17b;
  John 15:13; 1 John 3:13-18

What about those who are not my friends?
- Matthew 5:44—How am I to respond to those with whom I do not share a compatible relationship?
- Romans 12:17-21—How am I to treat those who are not my friends?
  Suggested Scriptures for your questions: Psalm 143; Proverbs 25:21-22

How am I to treat my fellow Christians?
- Romans 12:10—How should I treat other Christians?
- Romans 14:10-13—What must I guard against with fellow Christians?
  Suggested Scriptures for your questions: Matthew 7:1-2, 5; Philippians 2:3-4

What does Scripture teach me about making amends?
- Matthew 6:12-15—When others have wronged me, what must my attitude be?
- Matthew 5:23-24—When I have wronged others, what steps am I to take?
  Suggested Scriptures for your questions: Matthew 18:21-22; James 5:16

Am I ready for a heart search?
- Mark 11:25-26—Is there someone I am holding a grudge against?
- Luke 6:37-38—Am I self-righteous or judgmental?
  Suggested Scriptures for your questions: Matthew 5:38-42; James 3:13-17

Producing a profuse rose garden begins with the purchase of a variety of healthy plants, sustaining them with careful irrigation and nutrition, pruning when appropriate, and weeding regularly. Though your favorite color of rose in your friendship garden is a personal preference, each color, according to All American Rose Selections,[48] expresses a specific sentiment. As you consider the qualities resident in the friendship you extend to others in light of the following table, would you conclude that you have cultivated a multicolored friendship bouquet?

Color and Symbolism of Popular Roses	
COLOR	SYMBOLISM
Red	Love, respect
Deep pink	Gratitude, appreciation
Light pink	Admiration, sympathy
White	Reverence, humility
Yellow	Joy, gladness
Orange	Enthusiasm, desire
Red and yellow	Gaiety, joviality
Yellow	Sociability, friendship

As you consider the response to this question, perhaps the bit of prose that follows will assist you in affirming those you consider a part of your friendship garden.

Love

I love you not only for what you are,
but for what I am when I am with you.

I love you not only for what you have made of yourself,
but for what you are making of me.

I love you for the part of me that you bring out.

I love you for putting your hands into my heaped-up heart,
and passing over all the foolish and frivolous and weak things
which you cannot help dimly seeing there, and for drawing out into
the light all the beautiful, radiant belongings that no one else
had looked quite far enough to find.

I love you for ignoring the possibilities of the fool and weakling in me,
and for laying firm hold on the possibilities of good in me.

I love you for closing your eyes to the discords in me,
and for adding to the music in me by worshipful listening.

I love you because you are helping me
to make of the lumber of my life not a tavern,
but a Temple, and of the words of my every day
not a reproach but a song.

I love you because you have done more than any creed
could have done to make me good,
and more than any fate could have done to make me happy.

You have done it just by being yourself.
Perhaps that is what being a friend means after all.[49]

Developing a Gentle and Quiet Spirit

Scriptures to Study

    Matthew 7:1-5; Romans 14:4, 10-14; 1 Corinthians 4:3-5; 2
    Corinthians 13:5-6; James 4:11-12

For Meditation

    1 Corinthians 11:31

For Further Study

- Answer each question you wrote to aerate the soil of your friendship garden.

- Search the Scriptures for verses that align with the Symbolism column of the Color and Symbolism of Popular Roses table. Prepare your own table following the model below:

Color and Symbolism of Popular Roses		
COLOR	SYMBOLISM	SCRIPTURE REFERENCES

- The Queen of Sheba came to test Solomon with hard questions because she desired a heart of wisdom. Review 1 Kings 10, Proverbs 16:16, and Matthew 12:42. What qualities from her life would you ask your heavenly Father to integrate into yours?

A Principle to Ponder

    Precious in His sight is the woman who is more concerned about the quality of friendship she extends to others than what her friends can do for her (1 Samuel 18:4; 23:16-17).

Precious in His Sight is...
The Woman Who Purposes to Practice
Biblical Hospitality

*W*hether enjoying personal devotions, a Bible Study, or a worship service, what mental images emerge when you are presented with passages that encourage the practicing of hospitality? For many, they are based on the glossy photos in women's magazines—an immaculate home, a gourmet menu, and an exquisite table setting. While some of the photos could be applied to biblical hospitality, what they actually portray is entertaining.

When hospitality is described in the Scriptures, there is an absence of instructions relating to the home décor, menu, or table setting. Let's take a journey through Scripture as we paint a word portrait of biblical hospitality.

John 14:15 and 21-24 clearly state that the primary evidence that individuals are Christians is their choice to obey their heavenly Father's commands. Though we live in a world that promotes "have things your own way," to please your heavenly Father you need to respond to all of His instructions with an obedient spirit, not just pick those that appeal to you—and that includes our response to what His Word teaches about hospitality.

- Romans 12:13b says we that if you want to demonstrate obedience to your heavenly Father, you will practice hospitality.

- First Peter 4:9 reminds us that our attitude is of utmost importance. We are to practice hospitality without complaining. This verse challenges us to conduct a heart search to discern whether we are approaching this opportunity to minister with a hearty attitude (Colossians 3:23 NASB).

- Hebrews 13:2 is a reminder that our willingness to extend hospitality may have far-reaching implications. Abraham and Sarah (Genesis 18:1-3), Lot (Genesis 19:1-2), Gideon (Judges 6:11-24), and Manoah (Judges 13:6-20) all entertained strangers who were actually special messengers from God. While your motive should never be to give so that you will receive, Luke 6:38 states that the measuring cup you use to dispense your gifts and talents will be the same one used to provide your needs. What is the size of your hospitality-measuring cup?

- Third John 7-8 challenges us to extend hospitality to those involved in ministry for our Lord. It is exciting to know that as you share your home and resources with the Lord's servants, you become an active part of their ministry.

- One of the requirements for individuals involved in church leadership, according to 1 Timothy 3:1-2 and Titus 1:7-8, is a willingness to allow others to observe them in their homes—the arena where their character is most graphically revealed. Are you privileged to be in a leadership position in your church? If so, remember that these verses are requirements, not suggestions!

The attitude of the apostle Paul is one that all women who desire to cultivate a heart of biblical hospitality will want to copy. As you meditate on the scriptural passages we just studied, reflect on a time when you tried to extend friendship to others and were met with rejection. If you are like me, Satan uses rejection as a roadblock to prevent you from obeying your heavenly Father on future occasions.

Paul teaches that he moved toward his heavenly Father's will for his life—that of Christlikeness. He refused to dwell on the past or to drink of the cup of self-pity. Rather, he kept climbing higher toward his goal of Christlikeness all the days of his life. If we are to cultivate a heart of biblical hospitality, we must refuse to rely on past virtuous deeds and achievements or to dwell on sins and failures. We must lay aside past grudges and rejection experiences. We need to follow Paul's example and continue the ascent to the top of the "hospitality mountain." That ascent begins with developing proper climbing strategies. Here are some to get you started:

- Collect and file simple, inexpensive recipes for desserts and meals.
- Make a list of people who would be encouraged by your offer of hospitality. Purpose to invite your first guests soon.
- Start simple. Spontaneously inviting someone home after church is a great beginning.
- Pray that your loving heavenly Father will give you joy in demonstrating hospitality to others.
- Remember that memories require time and energy to create.
- Purpose to nurture a heart for biblical hospitality that sincerely communicates, "Come back soon."[50]

As I draw this chapter to a close, I want to share with you a word I coined to summarize its contents: *hospitalitude*. It is drawn from the word *hospitality*, meaning "to pursue the love of strangers" (Romans 12:13; Hebrews 13:2)[51] and *beatitude*, signifying the character of true faith. It is my prayer that this chapter stimulates you to practice biblical hospitality so that the *hospitalitudes* will be evident in your life.

Hospitalitudes[52]

Happy are those...

- who practice biblical hospitality, because in so doing they are demonstrating their love for God (1 John 3:17-18).

- who pursue the love of strangers, for they are obeying their heavenly Father's command and modeling His character (Romans 12:13b).

- in church leadership who practice hospitality, for they allow others to observe them in their homes, where their character is most graphically revealed (1 Timothy 3:1-2; Titus 1:5-8).

- who include people of all cultures on their guests lists, for in this manner they are demonstrating the expansive love of their heavenly Father (John 3:16).

- who are willing to make the sacrifice to practice hospitality, for they understand the importance of creating memories (Exodus 12:1-14).

- who develop hospitality management skills, for in this way they are being faithful stewards of all that our Lord has provided for them (1 Corinthians 4:2).

- who extend hospitality to "the others"—singles, widows, the grieving, the hospitalized, people with dietary challenges, and those experiencing food insecurity—for they are choosing to live out biblical compassion (James 2:14-16).

- whose homes are both a place of refuge and a center for evangelism, for they are glorifying their heavenly Father by their actions (1 Peter 2:11-12) and fulfilling His instructions "to do the work of an evangelist" (2 Timothy 4:5).

- who have consecrated their lives to their heavenly Father, for they are capable of practicing true biblical hospitality (2 Corinthians 4:7).

- who have consecrated their china to their Lord's service, for they have the opportunity of helping others to "taste and see that the Lord is good" (Psalm 34:8).

- who do not become disillusioned in practicing biblical hospitality, for they understand that in due time they will reap if they do not grow weary (Galatians 6:9).

- who acknowledge that they are unable to practice biblical hospitality in their own strength, for they know that our Lord's power overcomes their weaknesses and allows them to become vessels for His honor and glory (2 Corinthians 12:9-10; Philippians 4:13).

Developing a Gentle and Quiet Spirit

Scriptures to Study

> Romans 12:13b; 1 Timothy 3:1-2; Titus 1:7-8; Hebrews 13:2;
> 1 Peter 4:9; 3 John 7-8

For Meditation

> Hebrews 13:2

For Further Study

- Search the Scriptures to find how God used food in special ways to carry out His will and show His grace—for example, when Joseph sent his sons to Egypt to buy grain and thus found Joseph (Genesis 41-46).

- Evaluate your heart condition in relation to biblical hospitality.

  Write down several personal goals that will help you cultivate a hostess' heart.

  Pray that our loving heavenly Father will give you joy in demonstrating hospitality to others.

  Record your growth as you cultivate a hostess' heart.

- What do Genesis 18:1-3 and Hebrews 13:2 teach us about the results of the hospitality that Abraham and Sarah extended? What hospitality goals will you set based on their example?

A Principle to Ponder

> Precious in His sight is the woman who joyfully responds to His instructions to practice biblical hospitality (1 Peter 4:9).

The Godly Woman and Her Emotions
Precious in His Sight is the Woman Who:

20

Precious in His Sight is...
The Woman Who Assembles Her God-Given Assets

Do you ever feel like the hurrier you go, the behinder you get? Though difficult to believe, the real challenge is not the amount of time you have, but whether or not you have assembled your God-given assets (Matthew 25:1-30), committed them to Him (Romans 12:1-2), and trusted Him to multiply them (Philippians 4:13). As you think about assembling your assets, consider the most valuable one you possess, your time, and look at some basic facts about it:

- Everyone has the same amount of time (Genesis 1:3-5).
- God gives His children all the time they need (Philippians 4:19).
- If you are pressured by time, either you are doing the wrong things or you are doing the right things the wrong way (Proverbs 3:5-6).

If you are going to use time wisely, you must establish priorities and goals. The word priority implies that some things come before, or prior to, some others—not instead of. Priorities enable you to walk purposefully through life with guidelines for making decisions. God's plan of creation provides a priority model—He made animals and man when there was an environment to put them in (Genesis 1:6-27). Priorities provide incentive (Proverbs 29:18) and allow you to use time wisely so you are able to make a greater impact for the kingdom of God (Matthew 6:33-34). A Christian's priorities should reflect an eternal perspective and follow the model of the Lord, who glorified His Father while He was on earth by finishing the work His Father gave Him to do (John 17:4). David Livingstone eloquently describes this concept:

> I will place no value on anything I may possess except in relation to the Kingdom of Christ. If anything I have will advance the interests of that Kingdom, it shall be given away or kept, only as by giving or keeping it I may promote the glory of Him, to whom I owe all my hopes in time and eternity.[53]

Priorities assist us in setting goals—a result that requires action to achieve.[54] Strong people have goals; weak people only have wishes. If your life is going to significantly impact the kingdom of God, you will prayerfully establish goals. Proverbs 16:9 teaches that we should make plans, counting on God to direct us. Proverbs 23:23 encourages us to get the facts and hold on tightly to all the good sense we can get.

Elizabeth Goldsmith, a home management educator, writes, "In the greater scheme of life, goals are arranged in a hierarchy from fairly ordinary to extraordinary."[55] Writing down your goals and the steps required to accomplish them allows you to visualize the tasks before you and put them in order of their priority.

Numerous resources are available on time management. While they may offer helpful counsel and ideas, ultimately, each woman must learn what works for her. Generally a variety of techniques must be tried and customized for individual needs. If someone else's answers do not work for you, don't be discouraged. Here are some tactics that can assist you in assembling your assets:

- Dovetailing or Bunching—This strategy requires creativity since you are combining two or more activities and completing them simultaneously. For example, you might wash a load of laundry while doing a cleaning task close to the laundry area.

- Prayer is the most necessary yet habitually the most neglected tactic in the quest to sort priorities. Scripture teaches that God has promised to provide all of your strength and all of your needs (Philippians 4:13, 19). Without Him, you can do nothing (John 15:5), but with God, all things are possible (Luke 1:37). Taking the time to petition your heavenly Father to help you prioritize your responsibilities will multiply your time while reducing your stress level (1 Peter 5:7-8). Charles Hummel, in his classic booklet *The Tyranny of the Urgent*, places this tactic in perspective. "We know that Jesus' prayerful waiting for God's instructions freed Him from the tyranny of the urgent. It gave Him a sense of direction, set a steady pace, and enabled Him to do every task God assigned. And on the last night He could say, 'I have finished the work which thou gavest me to do.'"[56]

- Discern between the immediate and the urgent. There are many immediate but few urgent things, as the life of Paul Carlson clearly illustrates:

  Sometime ago, Simba bullets killed a young man, Dr. Paul Carlson. In the providence of God his life's work was finished. Most of us will live longer and die more quietly, but when the end comes, what would give us greater joy than being sure that we have finished the work that God gave us to do?[57]

- Distinguish between planning and control. A highly organized person can make things happen. When you are organizing you can be tempted to not remain dependent on God. That is why prayer must precede planning (Proverbs 16:3).

- Set aside time to plan. The time you save will far exceed the time you have spent in planning. And refuse to allow the urgent to take the place of the important in your life.

- Apply the following Planning Pointers:

    1. The longer the planning period, the less detailed the planning needs to be at the outset.

    2. Plan for the predictable. Leave ample time for the unexpected.

    3. Work smarter, not harder. Do difficult tasks when you're at your best, perform small tasks regularly to avoid bigger, more time-consuming jobs later, and delegate whenever you can.

    4. Think ahead. Do big projects piecemeal to avoid coming up short in the end since few things really have to be done at the last minute. Take time each evening to prepare for the next day.

    5. Don't trust your memory. Record priorities, plans, appointments, etc. on a calendar, then check it before making a commitment.

    6. Conserve and control time by establishing personal deadlines that occur before the actual deadline. Handling correspondence once, taming the cell phone or e-mails(they should be time-savers, not time-killers) and proctoring the three thieves of time—procrastination, perfectionism, and poor punctuality—can add hours to your days.

    7. Learn to live with loose ends.

    8. Reward yourself for completed tasks.

    9. Relax and enjoy life (John 10:10).

Your priorities, goals, and time are tools to allow you to fulfill the purposes that God has called you to—not your best friend's or next-door neighbor's. Going against your God-given assets depletes your energy and victimizes your time because you expend efforts in the wrong direction. Successful asset management depends on a sensible assessment of how you operate and what you can handle.

[handwritten margin note: God has called each person in a different way. So don't compare.]

The two things you should know about yourself in order to effectively embrace the successful management of your assets are your body cycles and your natural pace. Functioning within your body cycle allows you to maximize your most productive days and minimize your commitments on those days when your stamina easily wanes.

Dr. Hans Selye, the father of stress research, held that we all have a natural pace. Some people he likened to racehorses—fast and vigorous; others are like turtles—slow but sure. He warned against violating either bent. "The difference is inborn. If you force a turtle to run like a racehorse, it will die; if a racehorse is forced to run no faster than a turtle, it will suffer. Every person has to find his own best stress level, the highest level of activity that is pleasant for him."[58] If you know your assets and ask your heavenly Father to assist you in assembling them, you will be freed from the tyranny of the urgent so you can joyfully fulfill His will.

Developing a Gentle and Quiet Spirit

Scriptures to Study

>   Matthew 25:1-30; 2 Corinthians 4:1-18

For Meditation

>   Romans 12:1-2

For Further Study

- What is the role of prayer in establishing priorities and goals? (See 1 Samuel 12:23; Daniel 9:16-19; Matthew 6:9-10; John 14:13-14; Ephesians 6:18; 1 Thessalonians 5:17; James 5:16; 1 John 5:15.)

- In what ways has prayer impacted your life? If your life has not been impacted by prayer, why not?

- In what ways are you presenting yourself as a living sacrifice, holy and acceptable to God? How can you renew your mind? (See Romans 12:1-2.)

- Study the life of the widow who assembled her God-given assets and used them to glorify her heavenly Father (Mark 12:41:44; 2 Corinthians 9:6-8).

A Principle to Ponder

>   Precious in His sight is the woman who uses priorities, goals, and time as tools to fulfill God's plan for her life (Matthew 25:1-30).

21

Precious in His Sight is...

The Woman Who Chooses to Win Over Worry

*W*alk through a bookstore or pharmacy, or conduct an Internet search, and you will quickly see that worry, anxiety, and depression are prevalent maladies in twenty-first-century society. Research reports that 2 to 8% of the population suffer from General Anxiety Disorder (GAD). This is one of the major reasons people choose to visit a psychologist. Women tend to seek help twice as often as men. There is no specific age for the onset of GAD, yet research suggests that it commonly surfaces between the ages of twenty and forty. Symptoms include sweating, accelerated heart rate, dry mouth, stomach upsets, dizziness, and lightheadedness.[59]

Panic Disorder affects 1.7% of the US adult population between the ages of eighteen and fifty-four. Women are twice as likely to develop Panic Disorder as men. Panic Disorder causes people to feel terror suddenly and unexpectedly. Accompanying physical signs include dizziness, lightheadedness, rapid pulse, trembling, chest pains, shortness of breath, nausea, numbness, and a fear of going crazy or of dying. Panic Disorder can become debilitating when the person suffering begins to avoid situations or stimuli in which an attack is assumed to occur.[60]

While the medical terminology associated with worry, anxiety, and depression may be new, their incidence is as old as antiquity. Solomon's words "There is no new thing under the sun" (Ecclesiastes 1:9) accurately summarize the longevity of these ailments. Sarah and Hannah fretted about their barren wombs (Genesis 16:1-16; 1 Samuel 1:1-28). Naomi's anxiety caused her to develop a bitter spirit (Ruth 1:1-22). Job's wife's despair was so great that she counseled her husband to "curse God and die" (Job 2:9). Biblically the word care (*merimnao*) is used to describe anxiety, worry, and depression⁶¹—behaviors that divide the mind between worthwhile interests and damaging thoughts. The apostle James describes the miserable condition of the person with a divided mind. "A double-minded man [is] unstable in all his ways" (James 1:8). Worry generates many negative results and no positive ones. Those who worry allow themselves to become victims rather than victors over circumstances because they choose to rely on their own understanding rather than trusting in the timeless principles contained in the Word of God (Proverbs 3:5-6).

What is your reflex reaction when circumstances beyond your control occur? Do you worry or do you trust?

Just as good physical health is the result of implementing sound health practices, so good spiritual health is the result of applying sound spiritual practices. Let's take some time to examine your spiritual health. Answer each of the following questions using specific examples from your life.

As I attempt to maintain good spiritual health, do I...

1) • have the confidence that there is no good thing that God will withhold from me if I walk uprightly (Psalm 84:11)?

2) • believe God is able to do exceedingly abundantly beyond all I could ask or think because the Holy Spirit works within me (Ephesians 3:20)?

3) • trust that God will supply all my needs according to His riches and glory (Philippians 4:19)?

4) • ask in faith, without doubting, realizing that the one who doubts is unstable (James 1:6-8)?

5) have the confidence that the Lord will take care of my concerns, and thank Him for doing so (Psalm 138:8)?

6) believe that God cares for me because I am His child, and thank Him that I do not need to be anxious for tomorrow, since it will be taken care of by Him (Matthew 6:25-34)?

7) thank my heavenly Father that He gives me peace the world cannot give (John 14:27)?

8) refuse to waver in unbelief, but grow strong in faith, giving God the glory, being fully assured that what He has promised He is able to do (Romans 4:20-21)?

9) have confidence that if I ask for anything in God's will, He will hear me, but I can rest in the assurance that His will is always best for me (1 John 5:14-15)?

10) trust in the Lord with my whole heart, and refuse to lean on my own understanding (Proverbs 3:5-6)?

11) believe that I will accomplish much if I have faith and do not doubt (Matthew 21:21)?

12) focus on the reality that I have no reason to be anxious about what I shall eat, the clothes I need, or where I will live, because God will provide all these things for me? If God can take care of the birds of the air and the lilies of the field, why should I worry about my needs? Am I not more valuable than they (Luke 12:22-34)?

13) understand that it is impossible for me to be successful and please God if I lack faith (Hebrews 11:6)?

14) let Him have all my worries and cares, for He is always thinking about me and watching everything that concerns me (1 Peter 5:7)?

15) have the confidence that His grace is sufficient for me, for His power is perfected in my weakness (2 Corinthians 12:9)?

16) consider that it is God who is at work in me, both to will and to work for His good pleasure (Philippians 2:13)?

17) *   understand that I am not adequate in myself, but my adequacy is from God (2 Corinthians 3:5)?

18) *   believe that because I have been crucified in Christ, I no longer live, but Christ lives in me; and the life I now live, I live by faith (Galatians 2:20)?

If we desire to be spiritually strong, we will refuse to divide our minds with worry since it:

- does not accomplish anything (Psalm 37:8).
- is needless because God has everything under control (Matthew 6:31-33).
- can only be removed by prayer (Philippians 4:6-7).
- is a waste of time (Luke 12:25-26).

Worry divides the mind, but peace unites it. If you are to win over worry, anxiety, and depression, you must fix your mind on your heavenly Father, for only He provides perfect peace (Isaiah 26:3).

Developing a Gentle and Quiet Spirit

Scriptures to Study

> Joshua 1:9; Isaiah 26:3-4; 40:31; 55:6; Psalms 37:5, 7-8; 121: 2-5, 7-8;
> 145:18; Mark 11:23; Romans. 8:32, 37; 2 Corinthians 9:8; Philippians
> 4:6-8; James 5:16

For Meditation

> 1 Peter 5:7-8

For Further Study

- What biblical instructions can you find that will help you replace
  worry with trust? (See Joshua 1:9; Isaiah 26:3-4; 40:31; 55:6; Psalms
  37:5, 7-8, 121: 2-5, 7-8; 145:18; Mark 11:23; Romans. 8:32, 37; 2
  Corinthians 9:8; Philippians 4:6-8; James 5:16.)

- How will you use the responses from your spiritual health
  examination to consistently fix your mind on your heavenly Father?
  Write down several goals, then periodically record your progress
  toward them.

- Martha was rebuked by Jesus because of her choice to worry. Study
  her life and identify a positive potential for the negative character
  qualities that she exhibited (Luke 10:38-42). Do you have a tendency
  to worry? Apply what you learned from responding to this question
  to your life.

A Principle to Ponder

> Precious in His sight is the woman who chooses to cast all her
> anxiety, care, discontent, despair, and suffering on the Lord
> (1 Peter 5:7-8).

22

Precious in His Sight is...

The Woman Who Detonates Discouragement

When we speak of God answering our prayers, more often than not what we really mean is that He said yes to our petitions. One of the most challenging lessons for believers to learn is that yes, no, and wait are all responses to our requests. What is your reaction when you earnestly pray that a situation will have a specific outcome, and the response from your heavenly Father is no or wait? Do you believe that there is no good thing that He will withhold from you if you are walking uprightly (Psalm 84:11) and focusing on your responsibilities? Or are you like Elijah, who fled from Jezebel to the wilderness, sat under a juniper tree, and wished to die (1 Kings 19:4)? The woman who chooses the response aligned with Psalm 84:11 embraces contentment, while the one who opts for an Elijah Effect is courting discouragement.

Discouragement, extracted from the Greek word *athumeo,* means "to be disheartened, dispirited, and discouraged."[62] It often occurs when there is a discrepancy between expectation and fulfillment. Discouragement's roots are planted in the soil of idealistic expectations, such as holding perfectionist standards for yourself and others, embracing impractical outcomes for the institutions you are associated with, and anticipating unrealistic benefits from work, leisure time, education, or marriage. The greater the discrepancy between hope and fulfillment, the greater the potential for discouragement. In many instances the emotion of discouragement is actually anger without enthusiasm. Anger for selfish reasons is sin (Psalm 4:4; Ephesians 4:32).

Discouragement was a reaction of many individuals recorded in Scripture. As believers we should learn from both their positive and negative responses to cope with discouragement in our own lives (1 Corinthians 10:6) and to offer encouragement to others (2 Corinthians 1:3-7). Consider the following examples:

- Cain, when God pronounced judgment upon him for the murder of Abel (Genesis 4:13-14).
- Hagar, after she was cast out of the household of Abraham because of Sarah's jealousy (Genesis 21:15-16).
- Moses, when he was sent on his mission to the Israelites (Exodus 4:1, 10, 13; 6:12), at the Red Sea (Exodus 14:15), and when the Israelites lusted for flesh (Numbers 11:15).
- The Israelites, because of the cruel oppression of the Egyptians (Exodus 6:9).
- Elijah following his flight from Jezebel (1 Kings 19:4).
- Hannah as she experienced infertility (1 Samuel 1-2).
- Job following the devastation in his life (Job 3:1-26; 17:13-16).
- David through multiple difficulties (Psalm 41 and 51).
- Jeremiah, who was called "the weeping prophet" (Lamentations 3:1-21).
- Jonah after he preached to the Ninevites (Jonah 4:3, 8).
- The mariners with Paul (Acts 27:20).

An analysis of Elijah's life (1 Kings 19:1-22; 2 Kings 2:1-10) provides us with biblical guidelines for detonating discouragement.

Elijah emerged from his experience at Mount Carmel a victor. The 450 false prophets of Baal were destroyed, and the calamity of drought and famine brought about by idol worship ended (1 Kings 18:18-46).

Regrettably, Jezebel did not share his enthusiasm over the victory. In fact, she was very angry (1 Kings 19:1-2). Instead of surrendering, as Elijah expected, she issued an ultimatum to him. "So may the gods to me and more also, if I do not make your life as the life of one of them by this time tomorrow." (1 Kings 19:3). Elijah's response is similar to that of many Christians. They observe God perform repeated miracles in their lives, then a bit of minor turbulence occurs and the downward spiral of the Elijah Effect sets in.

Here's a summary of what I call the Elijah Effect:

- A cycle of fear of others, or of specific circumstances, starts (1 Kings 19:1-2).
- The logical reaction is to run from the problem rather than facing it head on (1 Kings 19:3).
- Instead of meditating on God's faithfulness, faulty negative thinking begins (1 Kings 19:4).
- The faulty negative thinking is fanned by emotional and physical fatigue, which frequently produces discouragement (1 Kings 19:5-9).
- Discouragement yields false expectations and unrealistic attitudes regarding the responsibilities God calls us to assume (1 Kings 19:10).
- These false expectations and unrealistic attitudes can lead to the cultivation of self-pity (1 Kings 19:14).

An intervention for the downward spiral of the Elijah Effect must be applied to reverse the process. In Elijah's case, the intervention to renew his spirit included:

- Resting and relaxing. Too many times, when the Elijah Effect is set in motion, people increase their activity rather than reducing it (1 Kings 19:5-9).
- Seeking solitude to focus on communion with God (1 Kings 19:9-13).

- Using the Word of God as a sword to fight the source of discouragement, Satan (Ephesians 6:17). Acquiring God's truth and promises during times of refreshment enables us to engage confidently in battle. Psalms 33, 42, 43, and 71 teach us the hope we are to have in God. Lamentations 3:21-23 describes the downcast man who nevertheless relies on the steadfast love of the Lord. First Peter 1:13-21 challenges us to proclaim the faith and hope we can have in God through Jesus Christ. Romans 8:18-39 reminds us that nothing can separate us from God's love.

- Realizing that refreshment comes through resuming activity, since it allows us to focus our vision outward rather than indulging in self-pity. Balancing the quantity of time invested and the intensity of the activity will ensure that the Elijah Effect does not recur (1 Kings 19:15-18).

- Allowing friends to minister to us (Proverbs 17:17). Remember, it is as important to be a friend as it is to find one. We are to accept God's provision for relationships rather than imposing our expectations on them. Elijah and Elisha possessed a strong relationship. They were one in mind and purpose: to serve Jehovah God. They built many memories together because Elisha willingly ministered to Elijah, offering encouragement and affirmation. The loyal partnership that developed provided a companion to compensate for Elijah's discouragement. And when God was ready to take Elijah to heaven, Elisha succeeded him in his prophetic office (2 Kings 2:9, 13). Their adventures to Gilgal (2 Kings 2:1), Bethel (2 Kings 2:2), Jericho (2 Kings 2:3-4), and the Jordan River (2 Kings 2:6) are a reminder that memories require time and energy to create. This poses the question, "What blessings would Elijah and Elisha have been deprived of had either refused to accept God's provision?"

Are you a woman who chooses the Elijah Effect or embraces

contentment when faced with circumstances that could breed discouragement? Remember that godliness with contentment is great gain (Psalm 37:16; 1 Timothy 6:6), while despair plus discouragement equals spiritual disaster.

Developing a Gentle and Quiet Spirit

Scriptures to Study

1 Kings 18:1-22; 2 Kings 2:1-10

For Meditation

Isaiah 41:10

For Further Study

- Study the lives of Cain (Genesis 4:13-14), Hagar (Genesis 21:15-16), Moses (Exodus 4:1, 10, 13; 6:12; 14:15; Numbers 11:15), the Israelites (Exodus 6:9), Elijah (1 Kings 19:4), Hannah (1 Samuel 1-2), Job (Job 3:1-26; 17:13-16), David (Psalms 6, 51, and 130), Jeremiah (Lamentations 3:1-21), Jonah (Jonah 4:3, 8), and the mariners with Paul (Acts 27:20) in light of their response to discouragement. In what ways will their examples impact your life so that you avoid despair and discouragement?

- What is your reaction when you earnestly pray that a situation will have a specific outcome, and the response from your heavenly Father is no or wait? Do you believe that there is no good thing that He will withhold from you if you are walking uprightly (Psalm 84:11) and focused on your responsibilities? Or are you like Elijah when he fled from Jezebel (1 Kings 19:4)? Use specific examples from your life to respond to this question.

- Develop a personal intervention process to thwart the Elijah Effect in your life. Use the Scripture passages listed in this chapter as a foundation.

- Analyze the life of Abigail, the wise wife who refused to be discouraged by her husband's foolish actions (1 Samuel 25:3-42; 27:3; 30:5; 2 Samuel 2:2; 3:2-3; 1 Chronicles 3:1). Which of her character qualities will you ask your heavenly Father to integrate into your life?

A Principle to Ponder

Precious in His sight is the woman who refuses to activate the Elijah Effect when faced with challenging circumstances (Romans 8:18-39).

23

Precious in His Sight is...

The Woman Who Runs to the Roar

*I*f you walked into a room and the conversation stops, would you assume people were talking about you? Would your reflex reaction be fear of rejection—the source of which is the fear of man (Proverbs 29:25)? Or would you trust in your heavenly Father, who loves you unconditionally (Jeremiah 31:3)?

Fear is defined as "a distressing emotion aroused by impending danger, evil, pain, etc., whether the threat is real or imagined."[63] We live in a fear-dominated world. Serious illness, weight gain, financial reversal, old age, death, and rejection are all objects of fear that can cause a focus away from God and toward the circumstance.

Fear is not always negative. When you sense danger, fear usually stimulates you to fight or flee. However, the fear of what people will think is always a negative reaction. You are reversing the Great Commandment described in Matthew 22:36-40 and placing more focus on people (Leviticus 19:18) than on God (Deuteronomy 6:5). This reversal is a natural response because we meet many of our yearnings through loving and being loved by others—affirmation, encouragement, companionship, and provision of physical needs. But others' potential to expose, humiliate, shame, reject, ridicule, revile, attack, oppress, or harm us physically, mentally, or spiritually provokes the fear response. These consequences are not positive. The fear of man can:

- Hinder your relationships with others.
- Stifle your ability to think rationally.
- Rob you of joy.
- Contribute to indecisiveness.
- Reduce your productiveness.
- Create inner turmoil.
- Injure your relationship with God.

Since the fear of man produces such detrimental results, it seems reasonable to locate an antidote to it. Scripture repeatedly instructs believers to replace fear with the knowledge that God is sufficient to override our fears.

- The natural reaction to fear is panic—the antidote is to replace potential fear with trust in God (Psalm 56:3-4, 11).
- If you trust in the Lord, you do not need to fear man (Proverbs 29:25).
- You are commanded to refrain from fearing the reproach of men (Isaiah 51:7).
- Since God comforts you, why should you be afraid (Isaiah 51: 12-16)?
- You can be content in every circumstance because God has promised to never leave you or forsake you (Hebrews 13:5-6).

Scripture constantly urges God's children to trust rather than fear. Consider this account, which was shared by an African missionary about a herd of lions:

> *This particular story is about the old king. You see, a lion can only be the king as long as he is strong enough to hold his position—and there is always another lion trying to usurp it. Usually by the time the old king is replaced he does not have any teeth and only a few claws. His hair is*

matted, he has arthritis in the joints, and he no longer can fight to keep his position, so a younger lion becomes the new king.

However, the old king is not entirely useless—he still has a role in the herd when the lions go on a hunt. When the herd hunts, the old, mean-looking, ferocious lion stands on one side while the young hunter lions hide in the bushes on the opposite side. When the prey appears, the former king looks at it and begins to roar; the roar scares the prey so badly that it runs to the opposite side—right into the waiting jaws of the hunter lions that attack and destroy it. If the prey had run toward the roar, more than likely it would have been safe, since all the old lion had left was his roar.

Scripture teaches that your "adversary the devil walks about like a roaring lion, seeking whom he may devour. Resist him, steadfast in the faith" (1 Peter 5:8-9 NKJV). If we are to resist him, we must live according to the truth of God's Word (2 Corinthians 10:3-5; Ephesians 6:17). As you learn sound doctrine and obey His Word, you will find that fear is dispelled. Jesus defeated Satan on the cross, thus stripping him of his power and leaving him with his frightening but harmless roar (John 12:23-33; Colossians 2:11-15; Hebrews 2:14-15). If you are going to refuse to succumb to Satan's impotent roar, you must replace fear with God's Word (Psalm 119:11; Ephesians 6:10-20). Begin today by memorizing and meditating upon these truths:

- God is with you and will keep you wherever you go (Genesis 28:15).
- You should not fear or be dismayed, for the Lord goes before you. He will not leave you or forsake you (Deuteronomy 31:6, 8).
- God will provide divine power for the tasks He calls you to accomplish (Joshua 1:5).
- God will be with you throughout the assignment He has commissioned you to undertake (1 Chronicles 28:20).
- When God calls you into a difficult situation, remember that the battle is not yours, but His (2 Chronicles 20:15).

- When you are protected by your Savior's rod and staff, you do not need to fear any potentially threatening environment—even death (Psalm 23:4).

- Because the Lord is your light, your salvation, and the strength of your life, you have no need to fear (Psalm 27:1).

- When you are afraid, trust in God. This is an act of the will, not the emotions (Psalm 56:3-4).

- No person can subvert God's protection of you (Psalm 56:11).

- God has provided an intimate place of divine protection for you (Psalm 91:1-7).

- If you delight in God's commandments, you do not need to fear evil tidings (Psalm 112:1, 7).

- Fear is removed when you reside in God's wisdom (Proverbs 3:25-26).

- You need not fear if you are God's child, because He is faithful to sustain you (Isaiah 41:10-13).

- Your sovereign heavenly Father controls even the most mundane events. Therefore you can have confidence that He will care for you (Matthew 10:29; Luke 12:6-7).

- The peace that your heavenly Father gives provides comfort in the midst of turmoil (John 14:27).

- If you are a child of God, you do not need to fear death or final punishment (Romans 8:14-16).

- Spiritual resources, seeking the welfare of others rather than your own, and a properly prioritized mind are gifts from your heavenly Father (2 Timothy 1:7).

- He who fears has not been made perfect in love (1 John 4:17-18).

The only positive fear recorded in Scripture is the fear of God. This is a reverence for God's majesty, power, and greatness. As you embrace the biblical definition of fear, the influence of the fear of man will dissipate.

Developing a Gentle and Quiet Spirit

Scriptures to Study

2 Chronicles 17:3-10, 20

For Meditation

Proverbs 29:25

For Further Study

- Develop a biblical description of godly fear. (See Isaiah 8:13; Proverbs 8:13; Job 28:28; Psalms 19:9; 111:10; Proverbs 14:27; 15:16; Hebrews 12:9, 28.)
- Create a biblical antidote to fear by responding to the statement "When I am afraid, I will . . ." (Psalm 56:3). Write the antidote on a card, carry it with you, and meditate on it when you encounter fearful circumstances.
- How does Esther, a woman who chose to run to the roar (Esther 4:1, 5-16; 7:1-6; 8:15-17), serve as a role model for you?

A Principle to Ponder

Precious in His sight is the woman who allows trust in her heavenly Father to be her natural response when faced with fear (Psalm 56:3, 11).

24

Precious in His Sight is...
The Woman Who Views Her Worth
Through the Grid of Scripture

The glossy, full-color magazine catches your eye at the grocery store checkout counter. As you thumb through it, you are once again confronted with the world's propaganda. It tells you that your worth is based on such external attributes and possessions as affluence, a lucrative profession, the perfect body shape, gorgeous hair, a spacious home, a luxurious car, and designer clothes. According to the media, these things will provide happiness, and when you are happy you will be a woman of worth.

When asked what one of the deepest longings of their hearts is, most women will quickly respond, "Happiness." The culture of the twenty-first century relentlessly seeks happiness, only to find it an elusive goal. David G. Myers, a social psychologist, describes this quest:

> *When we pit happiness against many things that we long for—robust health, social respect, large incomes—most of us choose happiness. Indeed, our search for happiness and for relief from misery motivates a host of behaviors, from success seeking to sex to suicide.*[64]

What would be your response if you were asked the following questions?

Do you...

- believe that you were fearfully and wonderfully made (Psalm 139:14-16)?
- argue with your Maker about your appearance, material possessions, or professional positions (Isaiah 45:9-11)?
- consider that you were created for God's glory (Isaiah 43:7)?
- live a lifestyle that declares God's praise (Isaiah 43:21)?
- question God about His purpose for the circumstances of your life (Isaiah 64:6-8; Jeremiah 18:3-16; Romans 9:20-29)?
- rejoice that God selected you to be a part of His family (1 Thessalonians 1:4)?
- comprehend that you are God's workmanship (Ephesians 2:10a)?
- bear in mind that you were created for good works (Ephesians 2:10b)?
- visualize that you are growing into a finished product (Philippians 1:6)?
- consider that the struggles you experience as a Christian, if responded to in a godly manner, will produce strength of character in your life (1 Peter 5:10)?
- contemplate that God has worthwhile tasks for you to accomplish until He comes for you or calls you home (Psalm 92:14)?

The feminist movement of the 1970s profoundly influenced the definition of happiness for twenty-first-century women by telling them that "justice for their gender, not wedding rings and bassinets,"[65] makes them happy and that women long for the freedom to "define themselves—instead of having their identity defined for them."[66] Today countless women maintain their quest for happiness and the anticipated feelings of self-worth outside the will of God. Only as they view their worth through the grid of Scripture will they find their deepest longings fulfilled. Consider the following comparison:

THE WORLD PROMOTES	GOD'S WORD PROMISES
Physical beauty yields compliments and praise.	"Charm is deceitful, and beauty is vain, but a woman who fears the Lord is to be praised." (Proverbs 31:30)
Performance yields significance or personal worth.	"I hated all my toil in which I toil under the sun, seeing that I must leave it to the man who will come after me." (Ecclesiastes 2:18)
Accumulation of wealth yields satisfaction.	"And I will say to my soul, 'Soul, you have ample goods laid up for many years; relax, eat, drink, and be merry.' But God said to him, 'Fool! This night your soul is required of you, and the things you have prepared, whose will they be?' So it is the one who lays up treasure for himself and is not rich toward God." (Luke 12:19-21)
Power and control yields gratification.	"Whoever would be great among you must be your servant." (Mark 10:43)
Professional prowess yields fulfillment.	"There was no end of all the people, all of whom he led. Yet those who come later will not rejoice in him." (Ecclesiastes 4:16).
Doing whatever you need to do to get ahead yields professional advancement.	"Whoever walks in integrity walks securely, but he who makes his ways crooked will be found out." (Proverbs 10:9)
Using people to reach your personal goals yields success.	"Let each of you look not only to his own interests, but also to the interests of others." (Philippians 2:4)
Finding the right marriage partner yields happiness.	"No good thing does he withhold from those who walk uprightly." (Psalm 84:11)
Promoting yourself yields personal fulfillment.	"Let another praise you, and not your own mouth; a stranger, and not your own lips." (Proverbs 27:2)
Asserting yourself yields fruitful results.	"Clothe yourselves, all of you, with humility toward one another, for 'God opposes the proud, but gives grace to the humble.' Humble yourselves therefore under the mighty hand of God so that at the proper time he may exalt you." (1 Peter 5:5-6)
Enhancing external attributes and amassing material possessions yield the abundant life.	"A thief comes only to steal and to kill and to destroy. I came that they may have life and have it abundantly." (John 10:10)

As you mediate on your responses to this comparison, how would you reply to the question "If you could change anything about yourself, what would you change?"

- Would your response echo that of the apostle Paul, who learned to be content in whatever state he was in (Philippians 4:11)?
- Would you consider that your unique traits, experiences, and personality were given to you by a loving heavenly Father for a specific work that will positively impact His kingdom?
- Would you acknowledge that the fulfillment of this ultimate purpose is left within your power since you are the one who must ultimately respond to your Creator?

Take a moment to consider the sum of your individual attributes. What do you think about them? Are you using each to further your heavenly Father's kingdom? Remember that as God's adopted daughter, your works are to reflect your Father's work in you (Matthew 5:16) and that your body is simply an earthen vessel used to store your inward character qualities (2 Corinthians 4:7). If you choose to cooperate with God on the development of character qualities that please Him, you will find yourself focusing on:

- your countenance—it should be pleasant (Proverbs 15:13).
- the cultivation of a gentle and quiet spirit, which is of great value to God (1 Peter 3:1-6).
- developing the qualities inherent in love (1 Corinthians 13:4-8).
- manifesting the fruit of the Spirit (Galatians 5:22-23).
- growing in your faith (2 Peter 1:5-7).
- gratitude—the act of the will that gives thanks to God for all that He has given you (Ephesians 5:20; 1 Thessalonians 5:18).
- behaving like His child (Colossians 3:12-17).

Rather than evaluating your worth against the fluctuating standards of the world, direct your energy toward your character first. Then you will truly be a woman of worth!

Jesus gave the two most important commandments related to your worth as a woman to a young lawyer who asked, "Teacher, which is the great commandment in the Law?"

Jesus responded, "'You shall love the Lord your God with all you heart and with all your soul and with all your mind. This is the great and first commandment. And a second is like it: You shall love your neighbor as yourself.'" (Matthew 22:36-39). As you maintain a dynamic relationship first with your Lord, and then with others, you will find lasting happiness and experience a genuine sense of worth that is based on the unchanging standard of God's Word rather than the propaganda of the world.

Developing a Gentle and Quiet Spirit

Scriptures to Study

    Psalm 37:3-4; Jeremiah 45:5; 7:9-11; 16:25; John 10:10; 15:11;
    James 1:17

For Meditation

    Matthew 6:25-27

For Further Study

- Study Hebrews 11, the "gallery of faith," and list each individual recorded. Determine their spiritual failures, then respond to the question "If God would use the individuals recorded in Hebrew 11, who experienced spiritual failures, why wouldn't He use me?"

- Take the time to prayerfully study the Scriptures and respond to the "Do You" questions contained in this chapter.

- Deborah was a woman whose heart was set on God (Judges 4-5). As you investigate her life, what qualities do you find? Which would you like to cultivate in your life? Ask your heavenly Father to assist you in assimilating them. Record your progress, and be sure to offer gratitude to Him.

A Principle to Ponder

    Precious in His sight is the woman whose sense of worth is based on the unchanging standard of God's Word rather than the propaganda of the world (Isaiah 43:21; 2 Corinthians 4:7).

25

Precious in His Sight is...
The Woman Who Embraces Forgiveness

*I*t's Mother's Day, and the pastor announces the Scripture text for his sermon: Proverbs 31:10-31. Inwardly you groan. *Oh, great. I am going to leave today's service on another guilt trip rather than encouraged and edified. Perhaps I can plan my week's menus or work on my Bible study while appearing to look interested.*

He begins his sermon by stating that Proverbs 31:10-31 introduces a woman whose lifestyle, values, and character align with the Word of God. This timeless passage paints a word portrait of a woman whose life we twenty-first-century Christian women are challenged to emulate. The immutability of God is in question if Proverbs 31:10-31 is not relevant.

Before studying the principles suggested in the Proverbs passage, he suggests that we look at six attributes of God:

- God's life does not change.
- God's character does not change.
- God's truth does not change.
- God's ways do not change.
- God's purposes do not change.
- God's Son does not change.

Since God does not change, then fellowshipping with Him, trusting in His Word, living by faith, and embracing His principles are essentially the same realities for twenty-first-century believers as they were for those of the Old and New Testaments.[67]

The description of the godly woman of Proverbs 31:10-31 is not designed to give women an inferiority complex. Rather, it provides a biblical foundation for the creation of principles by which the woman who desires to be considered precious in God's eyes prioritizes her life.

Eleven principles inspire the woman seeking to develop the fine art of godliness. She is virtuous, trustworthy, energetic, physically fit, economical, unselfish, honorable, lovable, prepared, and God-fearing.[68]

But you've heard all this before. And you never seem to measure up. That's why you try to "zone out" on the pastor's sermon. But several words from the pulpit catch your attention.

Your pastor asks you to take a moment to reflect on the heart of the eleven principles of the Proverbs 31 woman.

1. *Virtuousness* (31:10) is an inner quality that instinctively demands respect. Moral excellence characterizes this woman's behavior (Ruth 3:11).

2. *Trustworthiness* (31:11-12) is the ability to keep another's confidence. A wise woman's speech is encouraging, sympathetic, and tactful (Proverbs 25:11). Her love of her Lord is evident (John 14:15) and dependability is exhibited in her lifestyle (Proverbs 25:23).

3. *Energetic* (31:13-16, 19, 24, 27) suggests that a wise woman is a worker and not a shirker (Proverbs 10:4). Her Christianity is practical (James 1:17). She enjoys her work (John 4:36) and attacks it with a cheery attitude (Colossians 3:17).

4. *Physically Fit* (31:17) reminds us that to perform our duties efficiently we must be healthy. As wise women in progress, we seek to understand our personal limitations and then work within them (1 Corinthians 6:19).

5. *Unselfishness* (31:18) is displayed in her willingness to share her most valuable asset—her time—with others. A wise woman is not so busy with her own affairs that she can't lend a helping hand to others. Her words bring comfort, hope, cheer, and, when necessary, correction to those who touch her life (Galatians 6:10).

6. *Honorable* (31:25) is reflected in her choice to "stay away from every form of evil" (1 Thessalonians 5:22). She dresses modestly and understands the importance of maintaining a reputation of integrity (Proverbs 22:1).

7. *Lovable* (31:28-29) is manifested in the consistency of her lifestyle. She enjoys relationships that have depth because she seeks to sharpen her friends spiritually and intellectually (Proverbs 27:17).

8. *Preparedness* (31:21-22) allows a wise woman to cope with unforeseen circumstances with confidence (Philippians 4:13).

9. *Prudent* (31:26) implies that a wise woman is careful of the consequences; that is, she is cautious. When she speaks, she can be firm, yet kind (Proverbs 27:9b).

10. *God-fearing* (31:30) suggests that her actions and lifestyle consistently reflect that she stands in awe of her Lord (Proverbs 1:7) and loves Him with all her heart (Matthew 22:37).

Proverbs 31:31 describes the reward of cultivating these eleven principles. It tells us that a wise woman receives her rewards "in the gates,"(Proverbs 31:23) which refers to the public assembly of people. She is often rewarded in this life and always in the hereafter (1 Corinthians 3:10-15; 4:1-51; 1 Corinthians 5:10; Revelation 22:12). Jesus said, "You have been faithful over a little; I will set you over much." (Matthew 25:21). He who is faithful in serving the Lord here will be rewarded with an honored position in His millennial kingdom.[69]

A godly woman lives in such a way that Jesus' words in Matthew 25:21 characterize her daily life.

Your pastor then transitions to his next point: "A godly woman chooses to embrace forgiveness."

Sounds great, you muse. Then the martyr video begins to replay. You surrendered your life as a living sacrifice to the Lord's service, and instead of receiving praise you were maligned, neglected, and unappreciated by the assembly.

Your pastor says that you have two options when someone wounds you: develop a bitter spirit, or choose to forgive. Difficult as it is, our Lord's teachings direct us to forgive others—even when they don't deserve it (Matthew 6:14-15).

Forgiveness is denoted in the Old Testament by words that mean "send away," "cover," "remove," and "wipe away." In the New Testament, "send away" is used most often. The concept of forgiveness is also communicated by words that mean "to loose" (Luke 6:37), "be gracious to" (Luke 7:43; 2 Corinthians 2:7), and "pass over" (Romans 3:25). The Bible records human sinfulness, God's eagerness to forgive, and frequent calls by the prophets, Jesus, and Jesus' followers for repentance from sin and a return to God.[70]

The Scriptures paint a magnificent word portrait of God's forgiveness. Nehemiah 9:17 portrays God as being "ready to pardon, gracious and merciful, slow to anger, abundant in kindness" (NKJV) Exodus 34:6-7 compares God's response to the penitent and impenitent sinner. The psalmist offers the imagery that "as far as the east is from the west, so far has he removed our transgressions from us" (Psalm 103:12 NKJV). Isaiah describes God as casting all the prophet's sins behind his back (Isaiah 38:17) and forgetting Israel's sins (Isaiah 43:25). The vivid language of Jeremiah 31:34 and Micah 7:19 emphasizes the completeness of God's forgiveness. When He forgives, men's sins are dealt with thoroughly. God remembers them no more!

A godly woman seeks to incorporate God's gracious response and her Lord's model (Luke 23:34) into her own biblical method for forgiving others as well as seeking others' forgiveness. Scriptural principles that contribute to the formulation of a "forgiveness formula" include:

- Nehemiah 9:17—Our God is a God of forgiveness.
- Psalm 86:5—All who call on the Lord will be forgiven.
- Matthew 18:22—Forgiveness is to be unlimited.
- Mark 11:25-26—Forgiveness needs to be unilateral and unconditional.
- Luke 17:4—Forgiveness should be granted unendingly.
- Luke 23:43—Christ set the example of forgiveness.
- Colossians 3:13—I am to forgive as God in Christ has forgiven me.

The Scriptures used to create this godly woman's "forgiveness formula" confront her with the immeasurable forgiveness she receives from God. That forgiveness is to overflow into the lives of those who wrong her. She focuses on the importance of forgiving others from her heart and the need to work toward reconciliation whenever possible (Matthew 5:23-24). Acknowledging that it is not God's plan for her to seek revenge—He reserves that for Himself (Hebrews 10:30)—she refuses to develop a bitter spirit (Hebrews 12:14-16). Since God commands us to forgive others, refusing to do so is an act of disobedience against Him.

Equally important to forgiving others, the godly woman acknowledges that at times she will need to seek the forgiveness of those she has wronged. Adam and Eve (Genesis 3:9-12) demonstrate the unbiblical response to sin ...blame someone else!

It is our responsibility to assume personal blame for our part in a transgression (James 5:16), to seek the Lord's forgiveness (1 John 1:9), and to pursue reconciliation (Matthew 5:23-24). Phrasing such as "I was wrong when I (fill in the offense). Will you forgive me?" allows us to accept personal responsibility without casting blame on the offended person. Such a response demonstrates humility and fear of the Lord (Proverbs 8:13).[71]

Your pastor phrases the question, "Do you desire to be a godly woman?"

You bow your head and consider the implications of his message. *Do I believe that Proverbs 31:10-31 is relevant to me? Am I willing to formulate and apply a "forgiveness formula" to my life?*

Your response to these questions determines whether you desire to be a woman who is precious in His sight.

The sermon is over. The recessional begins. You leave the church encouraged and edified.

Developing a Gentle and Quiet Spirit

Scriptures to Study

Ruth 1-4

For Meditation

Colossians 3:13

For Further Study

- Using the format below, prepare a chart that allows you to set personal goals for the eleven principles embraced by the woman seeking to develop the fine art of godliness.

  __Your Name__, Godly Woman in Progress

PRINCIPLE AND PERSONAL DEFINITION	VERSE	PERSONAL GOALS
Virtuous. Wise. Aware of the consequences.	Proverbs 31:30	1. Place everything I read, view, or listen to through the grid of Philippians 4:8-9.

- Search the Scriptures to develop the thought that you are to forgive as your heavenly Father forgives you. List the verses you find, then use them to create your own biblical method for forgiving others.
- Ruth is the only person in the Bible who is called a virtuous woman (Ruth 3:11). As you read about her life (Ruth 1-4), use the chart below to define why this was an accurate description of her.

PRINCIPLE AND PERSONAL DEFINITION	VERSE	PERSONAL GOALS
Virtuous.	Ruth 1:16-18	Remain faithful to the commitment she married into

A Principle to Ponder

Precious in His sight is the woman who, when she is maligned, neglected, and unappreciated, chooses to forgive (Luke 23:34).

Epilogue

*A*s you may recall from the Introduction, *Precious in His Sight* was designed to allow you to spend time in your heavenly Father's company, cultivating character qualities that contribute to the development of a gentle and quiet spirit. The topics for the chapters were drawn from the spiritual challenges that I, as well as women I have taught and counseled through my spiritual pilgrimage, confront. As the unchanging Word of God is applied to our lives, we become victors rather than victims—and in the process we experience growth toward a gentle and quiet spirit.

Early in my teaching ministry I was amazed to discover that my students thought I was teaching conceptually rather than experientially. That's because I'd been reluctant to spend valuable class time talking about myself. Then one day a young woman walked into my office and stated, "I don't know why I am here to talk with you. I have many personal challenges in my life, and I need someone to counsel with me. But I don't think you would understand since your life has always been so perfect." As she poured out her heart to me, I felt as if I were looking in a mirror. Her life experiences almost exactly paralleled mine. I realized then that

I needed to explain that much of what I taught was the result of lessons I had learned from my heavenly Father. Perhaps what I shared with that woman about the seasons of my life will encourage you.

The Season of Divine Protection

I was abandoned by my birth parents. When my mother left the hospital, I stayed there.

During the first six months of my life, I battled pneumonia. Though I was unaware of my heavenly Father's presence, His promises to be a "father of the fatherless" and to provide "homes for those who are deserted" (Psalm 68:5-6) were functioning in my life.

Six months later I was adopted into a Christian family. At the age of ten, I learned in vacation Bible school that salvation was like being adopted into God's family. It was God's plan that the specialness of my first adoption would make me eager to become His daughter.

In the season of divine protection, my heavenly Father was faithful. Though you may not always feel your heavenly Father's presence, since you are His dear child, He will never leave you or forsake you (Hebrews 13:5).

The Season of Reinforcement

My church taught salvation each Sunday but did not teach me how to grow as His child. So I carried the burden of sick parents and many challenges, rather than casting my cares on Him (1 Peter 5:6-8). The death of my parents—my father when I was eighteen and my mother when I was twenty-three—was no surprise to God.

In the season of reinforcement, my heavenly father was faithful. He made Hebrews 13:5-6, "I will never leave you nor forsake you," a reality in my life.

The Season of Growth

My heavenly Father led me to Scott Memorial Baptist Church. There, under the ministry of Pastor Tim LaHaye, He confronted me with my sin. He showed me through His Word that I must repent of the sin, trust in Jesus for salvation, and submit to Him as Lord (Romans 10:9). I agreed with His declaration that Jesus is Savior and Lord (Romans 10:10), and thus had my salvation confirmed (Romans 10:13).

In the season of growth, my heavenly Father was faithful.

The Season of Spiritual Reproduction

From the date of that commitment, I have daily sought God's guidance. I desire to "walk by the Spirit" so I "will not gratify the desire of the flesh" (Galatians 5:16). I gladly responded to Him, as Mary did when she said, "Behold, I am the servant of the Lord; let it be to me according to your word." (Luke 1:38), by serving Him full time in Christian higher education for the majority of my professional career. He knew I could serve Him more effectively as a single woman, and He has consistently provided for all of my spiritual, physical, and emotional needs (1 Corinthians 7:7-8; Philippians 4:19). One day He will welcome me to heaven because I am His daughter and I will be coming home.

In the season of spiritual reproduction, my heavenly Father continues to be faithful.

As we conclude our study together, may I encourage you to record the seasons of your life and God's faithfulness to you so that when He welcomes you home, He will affirm you for your development, through His nurturing, of a gentle and quiet spirit (1 Peter 3:4).

Developing a Gentle and Quiet Spirit

- Return to the spiritual inventory located in chapter nine. Review the questions and your responses. What growth toward the cultivation of a gentle and quiet spirit do you observe? Pause to offer a prayer of praise to your heavenly Father for the good work He is continuing to perfect in you (Philippians 1:6).
- Record the seasons of your life and God's faithfulness to you.

A Principle to Ponder

Precious in His sight is the woman who consistently mediates upon her heavenly Father's faithfulness throughout the seasons of her life (Psalm 103).

Guidelines for Developing a Gentle and Quiet Spirit

Some practical steps to get yourself started in the direction of experiencing visible growth toward the development of a gentle and quiet spirit include:

- Communicate to your heavenly Father that it is your desire to regularly spend time with Him through the study of His Word and prayer.

- Consider sharing your commitment with someone who will frequently ask you about your personal time with Him.

- Decide on the best format to respond to each chapter's follow-up activities. Remember that writing about what you are learning helps you gain ownership with the content. You may want to create a form and then print multiple copies, or write your responses in a journal.

- Set yourself up for success by collecting the necessary tools to experience a productive time of study. Though needs will vary for each individual, some common items are:

A devotion notebook or journal—You will want to record your thoughts in a place where they can be referred to at a later date.

Your Bible—Always keep it where you study to avoid a scavenger hunt when it's time to commune with your heavenly Father.

Your copy of this book, Precious in His Sight.

A supply of pencils, pens, and other tools (such as a highlighter). You may find it handy to store them in a zipper pouch.

Index cards for your meditation verses and Principles to Ponder. You may also want a notebook ring to keep your meditation and principle cards together.

Post-it notes for reminders, especially for extraneous thoughts that distract your mind. (Write these thoughts down so you won't forget them, but don't allow Satan to impair your time with your heavenly Father by diverting your attention.)

A basket, box, or other container to store your tools. Graciously inform your family that this box is off limits to them so that you always have the supplies you need.

- Begin your time with your heavenly Father by asking Him to open your heart to the message He wants you to receive from your time with Him. Don't be in a hurry to move to the reading or written responses.
- Read the chapter. Record those thoughts that are important to you.
- Read the suggested "Scriptures to Study." I purposely did not include the wording of the verses in this book so that you would be encouraged to read and study them in your Bible.
- Divide the "Developing a Gentle and Quiet Spirit" activities into realistic segments. Writing about what you learned can help you remember and implement into your life what you read.

For Meditation. Psalm 119:11 teaches us that hiding God's Word in our hearts is the most effective weapon to prevent us from sinning.

- Read each verse from your Bible.
- Write the verse on one of your index cards. If you are artistic you might enjoy embellishing it at another time.
- Place the card in a prominent place so that you are frequently reminded of its content.
- Record each time you use the verse to thwart Satan's attacks. Write the occasion and the results on the back of the card (2 Corinthians 10:3-6; Ephesians 6:17; Hebrews 4:12).

Meditate (continually think about or contemplate) upon the Scriptures and your comments throughout the year, focusing on your heavenly Father's faithfulness to you.

A Principle to Ponder. A *principle* is "an accepted or professed rule of action or conduct."[72] Each chapter contains a principle that begins with "Precious in His Sight Is the Woman Who . . ." This is designed to direct your attention to the thoughts that are pleasing to our heavenly Father (Philippians 4:8-9). Follow the instructions for your verse meditation to create the Principles to Ponder cards.

A sample worksheet is located at the conclusion of these guidelines should a notebook version best fit your learning style. Be sure to adapt it to your needs.

Worksheet Sample

Chapter (insert number)

Precious In His Sight Is
The Woman Who (insert chapter title)

Scriptures to Study

For Meditation

Developing a Gentle and Quiet Spirit

A Principle to Ponder
Precious in His sight is the woman who...

Scripture Grids

The scriptural principles upon which the chapters of this book are built are given in the Scripture Grids on the next several pages.

The Godly Woman And Her Spiritual Life		
CH.	TOPIC, TITLE, AND PRINCIPLE	SCRIPTURE REFERENCES AND MEDITATION VERSES
1	TOPIC: Spiritual Nutrition TITLE: Precious in His Sight God Is the Woman Who Understands Her Physical and Spiritual Nutritional Requirements PRINCIPLE: Filtering daily decisions through the changeless instructions found in God's Word (Psalm 119:9-16).	SCRIPTURE REFERENCES: Deuteronomy 8:3; Psalm 119; Matthew 4:4; Luke 4:4; 2 Timothy 3:16. MEDITATION VERSE: Psalm 119:1
2	TOPIC: Spiritual Tests TITLE: Precious in His Sight Is the Woman Who Chooses to Be a Victor in the Midst of Tests PRINCIPLE: Choosing, in the midst of tests, to be a victor rather than a victim (James 1:2-5).	SCRIPTURE REFERENCE: Luke 1:26-47 MEDITATION VERSES: James 1:2-4
3	TOPIC: Spiritual Vitality TITLE: Precious in His Sight Is the Woman Who Cultivates Spiritual Vitality PRINCIPLE: Exhibiting spiritual vitality regardless of circumstances (Jeremiah 17:7-8).	SCRIPTURE REFERENCES: Psalm 1; Jeremiah 17:7-8 MEDITATION VERSES: Jeremiah 17:7-8

4	TOPIC: Spiritual Gifts TITLE: Precious in His Sight Is the Woman Who Joyfully Uses Her Spiritual Gifts PRINCIPLE: Adjusting the use of your spiritual gifts to your season of life (Ecclesiastes 3:1-22).	SCRIPTURE REFERENCES: Romans 12:3-8; 1 Corinthians 12:4-10; Ephesians 4:7-16; 1 Peter 4:7-11 MEDITATION VERSE: 1 Peter 4:10
5	TOPIC: Use of Spiritual Gifts TITLE: Precious in His Sight Is the Woman Who Is Willing to Be Stretched to Communicate God's Message of Hope to Others PRINCIPLE: Being both theologically sound and practically adept (James 1:21-25).	SCRIPTURE REFERENCES: Acts 18:18-19, 26; Ephesians 3 MEDITATION VERSES: Ephesians 3:20-21
6	TOPIC: Modesty TITLE: Precious in His Sight Is the Woman Who Wears Garments that Reflect Her Royal Heritage PRINCIPLE: Acknowledging that God's brand of modesty is always in style (1 Timothy 1:9).	SCRIPTURE REFERENCES: Deuteronomy 22:5; Proverbs 11:22; 31:21-25; Romans 12:1-2; 1 Timothy 2:9-10; 1 Peter 2:21-3:22. MEDITATION VERSE: 1 Peter 3:3
7	TOPIC: Singleness TITLE: Precious in His Sight Is the Woman Who Understands Singleness from Her Heavenly Father's Perspective PRINCIPLE: Using your days of singleness to concentrate on becoming complete in Christ (Colossians 3:10).	SCRIPTURE REFERENCES: Psalm 37:3-4; Proverbs 3:5-6; Jeremiah 29:11-13; 1 Corinthians 7:1-10, 32-34 MEDITATION VERSE:Psalm 84:11

8	TOPIC: Modeling Your Heavenly Father's Character TITLE: Precious in His Sight Is the Woman Who Models Her Heavenly Father's Character PRINCIPLE: Seeking to model our heavenly Father's character (Matthew 5:48; Ephesians 5:1; 1 Peter 1:15-16).	SCRIPTURE REFERENCES: Psalms 86, 145; Matthew 5:48; 1 Peter 1:15-16 MEDITATION VERSE: Ephesians 5:1
9	TOPIC: Spiritual Evaluation TITLE: Precious in His Sight Is the Woman Who Chooses to Evaluate Her Spiritual Growth PRINCIPLE: Regularly evaluating your spiritual growth (2 Peter 3:18).	SCRIPTURE REFERENCES: Ephesians 4:1-3; Philippians 1:6, 3:13; 4:6-9 MEDITATION VERSE: 1 Corinthians 11:31
The Godly Woman and Her Relationships		
10	TOPIC: Mentoring TITLE: Precious in His Sight Is the Woman Who Chooses to Be a Grateful Mentee PRINCIPLE: Being a maturing mentee who consistently expresses her gratitude to her mentor. (1 Thessalonians 5:18).	SCRIPTURE REFERENCES: Proverbs 17:17; Luke 1:39-56; 1 Corinthians 4:16; 11:1; Titus 2:3-5; 3 John 1:4 MEDITATION VERSE: Philippians 1:3-6
11	TOPIC: Impartiality TITLE: Precious in His Sight Is the Woman Who Embraces Impartiality PRINCIPLE: Seeking to fulfill "the royal law according to the Scriptures" and loving your neighbor as yourself (Matthew 22:37-40, James 2:8).	SCRIPTURE REFERENCE: James 2:1-17, Matthew 7:12; 22:34-39 Mark 12:8-34 MEDITATION VERSE: Proverbs 31:20

12	TOPIC: Spiritual Motherhood TITLE: Precious in His Sight Is the Woman Who Chooses to Be a Spiritual Mother PRINCIPLE: Joyfully embracing the Titus 2:3-5 principle.	SCRIPTURE REFERENCES: 1 Kings 22:51-52; Psalm 113:9; Isaiah 66:13; Ezekiel 16:44-45; 1 Timothy 2:9-12, 15; 5:14; 1 Peter 3:3-6 MEDITATION VERSE: Titus 2:3-5
13	TOPIC: Honoring Our Earthly Fathers TITLE: Precious in His Sight Is the Woman Who Honors Her Earthly Father. PRINCIPLE: Extending gratitude to both your heavenly and earthly father (1 Thessalonians 5:18)	SCRIPTURE REFERENCES: Exodus 20:12; Deuteronomy 5:16; Matthew 15:4; 19:19; Mark 7:10; 10:19; Luke 18:20; Ephesians 6:2 MEDITATION VERSES: Proverbs 1:8-9
14	TOPIC: Friendship TITLE: Precious in His Sight Is the Woman Who Offers Trust and Confidence in Her Friendships. PRINCIPLE: Nurturing your friendships—one of His most precious gifts to you (John 15:13).	SCRIPTURE REFERENCES: 1 Samuel 18:1-4; 19:1-7; 2 Samuel 1:26; 20:24-33; Luke 1:39-56 MEDITATION VERSE: Proverbs 17:17
15	TOPIC: Friendship TITLE: Precious in His Sight Is the Woman Who Acknowledges Her Need for Womanly Companionship PRINCIPLE: Acknowledging the need to cultivate female friendships (Ecclesiastes 4:9-12).	SCRIPTURE REFERENCES: Proverbs 18:24; 27:6, 9-10; John 13:34-35; 15:12-17; 1 John 4:7. MEDITATION VERSE: Ecclesiastes 4:9-12

16	TOPIC: Friendship TITLE: Precious in His Sight Is the Woman Who Cultivates Her Friendship Garden PRINCIPLE: Conscientiously cultivating your friendship garden (Ephesians 4:32; Galatians 6:1-2; 1 Thessalonians 5:14)	SCRIPTURE REFERENCES: Proverbs 31:11; Matthew 5:23-24; 6:14-15; Mark 10:25-26; John 13:35; Romans 12:10-13; 1 Corinthians 13; 2 Corinthians 9:6; Galatians 6:1, 7; Ephesians 4:31-32; 2 Timothy 2:23-26; 1 John 4:20-21 MEDITATION VERSE: Romans 12:10-13
17	TOPIC: Friendship TITLE: Precious in His Sight Is the Woman Who Weeds Her Friendship Garden PRINCIPLE: Consistently weeding your friendship garden (James 4:6).	SCRIPTURE REFERENCES: John 4, 17 MEDITATION VERSES: Ephesians 4:25-32
18	TOPIC: Friendship TITLE: Precious in His Sight Is the Woman Who Evaluates the Quality of Friendship She Extends to Others PRINCIPLE: Being more concerned about the quality of friendship you extend to others than what your friends can do for you (1 Samuel 18:4, 23:16-17)	SCRIPTURE REFERENCES: Matthew 7:1-5; Romans 14:4, 10-14; 1 Corinthians 4:3-5; 2 Corinthians 13:5-6; James 4:11-12 MEDITATION VERSE: 1 Corinthians 11:31

19	TOPIC: Biblical Hospitality TITLE: Precious in His Sight Is the Woman Who Purposes to Practice Biblical Hospitality PRINCIPLE: Joyfully responding to His instructions to practice biblical hospitality (1 Peter 4:9).	SCRIPTURE REFERENCES: Romans 12:13b; 1 Timothy 3:1-2; Titus 1:7-8; Hebrews 13:2; 1 Peter 4:9; 3 John 7-8 MEDITATION VERSE: Hebrews 13:2

The Godly Woman and Her Emotions

20	TOPIC: Priorities TITLE: Precious in His Sight Is the Woman Who Assembles Her God-Given Assets. PRINCIPLE: Using priorities, goals, and time as tools to fulfill God's plan for your life (Matthew 25:1-30)	SCRIPTURE REFERENCES: Matthew 25:1-30; 2 Corinthians 4:1-18 MEDITATION VERSE: Romans 12:1-2
21	TOPIC: Worry TITLE: Precious in His Sight Is the Woman Who Chooses to Win Over Worry PRINCIPLE: Casting all your anxiety, care, discontent, despair, and suffering on the Lord (1 Peter 5:7-8)	SCRIPTURE REFERENCES: Joshua 1:9; Isaiah 26:3-4; 40:31; 55:6; Psalms 37:5, 7-8,; 121:2-5, 7-8; 145:18; Mark 11:23; Romans 8:32, 37; 2 Corinthians 9:8; Philippians 4:6-8; James 5:16 MEDITATION VERSE: 1 Peter 5:7-8
22	TOPIC: Discouragement TITLE: Precious in His Sight Is the Woman Who Detonates Discouragement PRINCIPLE: Refusing to activate the Elijah Effect when faced with challenging circumstances (Romans 8:18-39).	SCRIPTURE REFERENCES: 1 Kings 19:1-22; 2 Kings 2:1-10 MEDITATION VERSE: Isaiah 41:10

23	TOPIC: Fear TITLE: Precious in His Sight Is the Woman Who Runs to the Roar PRINCIPLE: Allowing trust in your heavenly Father to be your natural response when faced with fear (Psalm 56:3, 11)	SCRIPTURE REFERENCE: 2 Chronicles 17:3–10, 20 MEDITATION VERSE: Proverbs 29:25
24	TOPIC: Worth TITLE: Precious in His Sight Is the Woman Who Views Her Worth through the Grid of Scripture PRINCIPLE: Basing your worth on the unchanging standard of God's Word rather than the propaganda of the world (Isaiah 43:21; 2 Corinthians 4:7)	SCRIPTURE REFERENCES: Psalm 37:3-4; Jeremiah 45:5; 7:9-11, 16:25; John 10:10, 15:11; James 1:17 MEDITATION VERSE: Matthew 6:25-27
25	TOPIC: Forgiveness TITLE: Precious in His Sight Is the Woman Who Embraces Forgiveness PRINCIPLE: Choosing to forgive when you are maligned, neglected, and unappreciated (Luke 23:34).	SCRIPTURE REFERENCE: Ruth 1-4 MEDITATION VERSE: Colossians 3:13

EPILOGUE

PRINCIPLE

Precious in His sight is the woman who consistently mediates upon her heavenly Father's faithfulness throughout the seasons of her life (Psalm 103).

Notes

[1] John MacArthur, *The MacArthur Study Bible* (Nashville: Word, 1997), note at 1 Peter 3:4, a gentle and quiet spirit.

[2] For further elaboration see Pat Ennis and Lisa Tatlock, *Designing a Lifestyle that Pleases God* (Chicago: Moody, 2004), chapter 10.

[3] John MacArthur, *The MacArthur Study Bible* (Nashville: Word, 1997), note at 1 Peter 2:2, desire the pure milk of the word.

[4] John MacArthur, *The MacArthur Study Bible* (Nashville: Word, 1997), note at James 1:5.

[5] *Webster's College Dictionary, 2nd ed.* (Random House, 1997), victim, victor.

[6] See J. Vernon McGee, *Bible Commentary* (Nashville: Thomas Nelson, Inc., 1977), 242-248.

[7] John MacArthur, *The MacArthur New Testament Commentary, Ephesians* (Chicago: Moody, 1986), 86-113. John MacArthur, The MacArthur Study Bible (Nashville: Word, 1997), 1801-2, 1806-1808.

[8] Boyd Munger, *My Heart Christ's Home* (Downer's Grove, IL: InterVarsity Press, 1992).

[9] John MacArthur, *The MacArthur Study Bible* (Nashville: Word, 1997), note at Ephesians 3:20.

[10] *Webster's College Dictionary, 2nd ed.* (Random House, 1997), modesty.

[11] For further elaboration see Pat Ennis and Lisa Tatlock, *Designing a Lifestyle that Pleases God* (Chicago: Moody, 2004), 221-257.

[12] John MacArthur, *The MacArthur Study Bible* (Nashville: Word, 1997), note at Numbers 15:37-38, tassels.

[13] For further elaboration see Pat Ennis and Lisa Tatlock, *Becoming a Woman Who Pleases God: A Guide to Developing Your Biblical Potential* (Chicago: Moody, 2003), 257.

[14] Bryan Strong, Christine DeVault, and Barbara Sayad, *The Marriage and Family Experience* (New York: Wadsworth Publishing Company, 1998), 172.

[15] For further elaboration see Pat Ennis and Lisa Tatlock, *Becoming a Woman Who Pleases God: A Guide to Developing Your Biblical Potential* (Chicago: Moody, 2003), 25-47.

[16] John MacArthur, *The MacArthur Study Bible* (Nashville: Word, 1997), note at Ephesians 5:1, be imitators of God.

[17] *Webster's College Dictionary, 2nd ed.* (Random House, 1997), great.

[18] For further elaboration see Pat Ennis and Lisa Tatlock, *Becoming a Woman Who Pleases God: A Guide to Developing Your Biblical Potential* (Chicago: Moody, 2003), 287-306.

[19] *Harper's Bible Dictionary* (San Francisco: Harper and Row, 1985), gracious.

[20] For further elaboration see Pat Ennis and Lisa Tatlock, *Becoming a Woman Who Pleases God: A Guide to Developing Your Biblical Potential* (Chicago: Moody, 2003), 145-6.

[21] *Webster's College Dictionary, 2nd ed.* (Random House, 1997), impartial.

[22] John MacArthur, *The MacArthur Study Bible* (Nashville: Word, 1997), note at James 2:1, partiality.

[23] John MacArthur, *The MacArthur Study Bible* (Nashville: Word, 1997), note at James 2:8, royal law.

[24] *Webster's College Dictionary, 2nd ed.* (Random House, 1997), single.

[25] "'I Do, I Do,' But Not Yet: More in America putting off marriage," *USA TODAY*, December 1, 2004, www.usatody.com/news/bythenumbers/2004-12-01-never-married_x.htm (accessed May 16, 2006).

[26] *Webster's College Dictionary, 2nd ed.* (Random House, 1997), widow.

[27] Found at www.aarp.org/griefandloss/articles/93_a.html (accessed November 21, 2003).

[28] For further elaboration see Pat Ennis and Lisa Tatlock, *Becoming a Woman Who Pleases God: A Guide to Developing Your Biblical Potential* (Chicago: Moody, 2002), 273-278.

[29] Found at www.lafightshunger.org/statistics.html (accessed November 21, 2003).

[30] Verna Birkey, *Women Connecting with Women* (Mukileto: WinePress, 1998), 54.

[31] W. E. Vine, *Vine's Expository Dictionary of Old and New Testament Words* (Grand Rapids, Mich.: Revell, 1981), "encourage."

[32] W. E. Vine, *Vine's Expository Dictionary of Old and New Testament Words* (Grand Rapids, Mich.: Revell, 1981), "admonition."

[33] John MacArthur, *The MacArthur Study Bible* (Nashville: Word, 1997), note at 1 Samuel 20:17, loved him as his own soul.

[34] A helpful resource is Elizabeth: Lessons on Grace and Faith from the Life of an Older Woman by Nancy Leigh DeMoss. (Visit the Revive Our Hearts Web site, http://www.LifeAction.org).

[35] Found at http://www.godstypist.com (accessed May 6, 2006). Used by permission.

[36] Kahlil Gibran, *The Prophet* (New York: Alfred A. Knoph, Inc., 1923), 58.

[37] Beverly LaHaye, *The Desires of a Woman's Heart* (Wheaton: Tyndale, 1993), 32.

[38] Lucy Maud Montgomery, *Anne of Green Gables* (New York: Grosset and Dunlap, 1935).

[39] Gale Berkowitz, "UCLA Study on Friendship Among Women," Natural Health California Newsletter, June 2003, http://wwwisismedica.com/Friendship%20and%20Health.htm (accessed January 10, 2005).

[40] *Webster's College Dictionary, 2nd ed.* (Random House, 1997), cultivate.

[41] Found at http://ad.backyardgardener.com (accessed January 13, 2005).

[42] John MacArthur, *The MacArthur Study Bible* (Nashville: Word, 1997), note at Galatians 6:10, especially...the household of faith.

[43] Verna Birkey, *Women Connecting with Women* (Mukileto: WinePress Publishing, 1998), 54.

[44] Found at http://www.blm.gov/weeds (accessed January 13, 2005).

[45] Found at http://www.blm.gov/weeds (accessed January 13, 2005).

[46] Found at http://www.blm.gov/weeds (accessed January 13, 2005).

[47] "Controlling Weeds," http://www.lowes.com (accessed January 13, 2005).

[48] Found at www.rose.org/site/epage/13599_429.html (accessed January 17, 2005).

[49] Roy Croft, *"Love," The Ideals Treasury of Best Loved Poems, ed. Patricia Pingry* (Nashville: Ideals, 1997), 95.

[50] For further elaboration see Pat Ennis and Lisa Tatlock, *Becoming a Woman Who Pleases God: A Guide to Developing Your Biblical Potential.* (Chicago: Moody, 2003), 171-187.

[51] John MacArthur, *The MacArthur Study Bible* (Nashville: Word, 1997), note at Romans 12:13, given to hospitality.

[52] © Pat Ennis, 2004.

[53] *The Navigators, Studies in Christian Living, Book 6, Growing in Service* (Colorado Springs: NavPress, 1969).

[54] Elizabeth B. Goldsmith, *Resource Management for Individuals and Families* (California: Wadsworth, 2005), 8.

[55] Elizabeth B. Goldsmith, *Resource Management for Individuals and Families* (California: Wadsworth, 2005), 7.

[56] Charles Hummel, *Tyranny of the Urgent* (Downers Grove, IL: InterVarsity, 1967), 9.

[57] Charles Hummel, *Tyranny of the Urgent* (Downers Grove, IL: InterVarsity, 1967), 12-15.

[58] Found at www.whonamedit.com/doctor.cfm/2538.html (accessed January 21, 2005).

[59] Found at www.anxietysecrets.com/anxpanic.html (accessed January 21, 2005).

[60] Found at www.anxietysecrets.com/anxpanic.html (accessed January 21, 2005).

[61] W. E. Vine, *Vine's Expository Dictionary of Old and New Testament Words* (Grand Rapids, Mich.: Revell, 1981), care, careful, carefully, carefulness.

[62] W. E. Vine, *Vine's Expository Dictionary of Old and New Testament Words* (Grand Rapids, Mich.: Revell, 1981), athumeo.

[63] *Webster's College Dictionary, 2nd ed.* (Random House, 1997), fear.

[64] David G. Myers, *The Pursuit of Happiness: Who Is Happy—and Why?*(New York: William Morrow and Company, 1992), 19.

[65] Susan Faludi, Backlash: *The Undeclared War against American Women* (New York: Crown Publishers, Inc., 1991), xvi.

[66] Susan Faludi, Backlash: *The Undeclared War against American Women* (New York: Crown Publishers, Inc., 1991), xvii.

[67] J. I. Packer, *Knowing God* (Downers Grove, IL: InterVarsity, 1973), 68-72.

[68] For further elaboration see Pat Ennis and Lisa Tatlock, *Becoming a Woman Who Pleases God: A Guide to Developing Your Biblical Potential* (Chicago: Moody, 2003).

[69] Tim LaHaye and Jerry B. Jenkins, *Perhaps Today: Living Every Day in the Light of Christ's Return* (Wheaton: Tyndale, 2001), 165.

[70] *Harper's Bible Dictionary* (San Francisco: Harper and Row, 1985), forgiveness.

[71] For further elaboration see Pat Ennis and Lisa Tatlock, *Becoming a Woman Who Pleases God: A Guide to Developing Your Biblical Potential* (Chicago: Moody, 2003).

[72] *Webster's College Dictionary, 2nd ed.* (Random House, 1997), principle.